LIFE TOUCHED WITH WONDER

LIFE TOUCHED WITH WONDER

THE GIFT *of* FRIENDSHIP

FROM THE EDITORS OF READER'S DIGEST

THE READER'S DIGEST ASSOCIATION, INC.
PLEASANTVILLE, NEW YORK

ISBN 0-7621-8870-7

Printed in the United States of America

Book design by Patrice Sheridan

You can also visit us on the World Wide Web at http://www.readersdigest.com

CONTENTS

INTRODUCTION

Men wonder at the height of mountains, the huge waves of the sea, the broad flow of rivers, the course of the stars—and forget to wonder at themselves.
— Saint Augustine

We feel awe when we see a grand landscape or view the majesty of a starry sky. But there's also wonder in a child's kiss when you're feeling down, in a friend's unexpected recovery from a frightening illness, in a walk on a hushed, snowy night. Such moments take us by surprise and lift us from the mundane and the familiar. Suddenly, inexplicably, we catch a glimpse of a reality beyond ourselves, and see evidence that there is something beautiful, merciful, loving knit into the fabric of creation—even in ourselves.

In fact, ordinary people can be the most gifted messengers of wonder. Their stories offer compelling evidence of the power of the spirit in daily life. In this new book series we have selected the best of such true-life stories and present them in separate volumes organized around themes.

In good times and bad, it is our friends who inspire us, comfort us, and see us through whatever surprises life throws our way. *The Gift of Friendship* shares the heartwarming stories of ordinary people whose lives have been touched in extraordinary ways by those they hold most dear— their friends.

A PLACE AT THE TABLE

BY

COLLIN PERRY

Alan Stoudemire stared nervously out of the car window at Lincolnton, North Carolina, where he'd grown up. The Colorado physician had returned before, to see his family, but this trip was different. After passing the old farmhouse that had been his boyhood home, the car pulled up in front of an unpainted one-story cottage. Across the lawn, Boyce Blake and his brothers were sitting around a card table, engaged in a game of bid whist.

Stoudemire hesitated. Despite the air conditioning, he was sweating profusely. It had been a long way to come, but for what? Could a friendship forged as kids be resurrected after all these years?

Sandy-haired Alan Stoudemire had first met Boyce Blake one summer day in the 1950s when both were about five. Alan was playing in the creek along the back of his parents' property, shoving a stick down interesting-looking holes in the embankment. He looked up to see a black boy gazing at him from across the creek, a basket of blackberries almost half his size slung over his shoulder.

"Don't you know those are water-moccasin nests?" asked the stranger.

While it was only the creek that separated the boys' rural Lincolnton homes, an ocean of prejudice and intolerance lay between them. Still, the two became inseparable. They hunted, fished and camped out together, with the sturdier, outdoor-savvy Boyce often showing his friend the way.

He began calling Alan "Zeke." "How come?" Alan asked.

"Guess you just look like a Zeke to me," Boyce explained. And among their friends, Zeke became his name.

The conservatively raised, religious Boyce usually took the more cautious role in their adventures. One day, despite his friend's warnings, Zeke got the idea of pouring gasoline down an abandoned well on his father's property and lighting it. The explosion hit Boyce full in the face and hurtled him onto his back.

Zeke's father quickly appeared on the scene, gathered up the bleeding boy and started for the house. "Better go get Miss Ruth" was all he said to his son. Zeke raced to get Boyce's mother.

"I'm sorry—it was my fault, ma'am," he said.

"Um, um, two little devils," said Miss Ruth, shaking her head. "I heard that explosion from way over our place."

Zeke's punishment was to spend the next month collecting rocks and dropping them, one by one, down into the 60-foot well to fill it. He hadn't been at it more than a day before there was Boyce, working beside him in the hot sun.

The Stoudemire farm was fertile, the house comfortable. Zeke enjoyed his own room, even his own horse.

Across the creek, the Blakes and their 12 children lived on a few unyielding acres in a cramped house with no running water. Yet with matriarch Miss Ruth presiding, the floor was always swept clean, the children neatly attired. They were among the few black families who owned their land—a concession by a local landowner to Mr. Blake's military service.

At first, the separate worlds that Zeke and Boyce inhabited seemed natural to them. But one summer the unfairness was driven home to both boys.

While white children played baseball on a groomed playground diamond, Zeke preferred to join his black friends on an improvised field in a pasture. One hot day, after a grueling nine innings, Zeke got on his horse to go cool off in the county's only pool. As he waved good-bye to his friends, he watched them passing around some warm Kool-Aid.

His friends were just as hot as he was, Zeke realized.

The pool was for war veterans, families and friends, but Boyce's father as well as his own had seen active combat in the Pacific in World War II. Zeke tied his horse at the gate, walked past the "Members Only" sign and asked the manager, politely, why he couldn't bring his black friends for a swim.

"Well, son, they're not members, are they?" said the manager.

Zeke nodded toward the pool. "Are all those white kids members?"

The manager's expression turned hostile. "What the hell business is it of yours, boy?"

Angrily, Zeke decided that if his friends couldn't swim, he wouldn't. As his horse splashed home over the creek, the boy had an idea. He galloped back to the ball field.

What if they dammed the creek and made a swimming hole? he asked excitedly.

It was tedious, exhausting work. The boys pitched in mud, rocks, logs, old tires—anything they could find. In a few days they'd fashioned a crude dam, backing up water deep enough to jump in after ballgames for the rest of the summer.

The years came and went, the dam was washed away each spring, and each summer was rebuilt by the boys. Each fall Zeke played football with Boyce and his friends. Growing tough and strong, he found he liked the roughhouse chasing, blocking and tackling—without helmets or padding—even more than the patient symmetry of baseball.

One Sunday after church, Boyce and his three brothers invited Zeke to play "bid whiz." Solemnly, Boyce told him, "No white boy's ever been let into the game before." Zeke joined in the high-speed whist, with its subtle bids and signals, while the Blakes gently kidded their inept new player. The card sessions became a weekly ritual.

In September 1968, integration was introduced to Lincolnton's all-white high school. Boyce, blinking in the morning light, stepped from the bus into a sea of sullen white faces. The black kids with him clumped together beside the bus, and the whites formed a circle around them. Both groups seemed frozen momentarily, and dangerously silent. The space between them was charged with tension and potential violence.

Zeke approached the outer ring of whites. Craning over their heads, he could make out Boyce standing with the other blacks. But something he saw in his old friend gave him a cold shudder; probably for the first time in his life, Boyce Blake seemed genuinely afraid.

"Excuse me, excuse me, please," Zeke said, nudging through the crowd. Then, alone and with all eyes focused on him, he crossed the short distance separating the two groups.

"Hey, man, I've been looking all over for you," said a nervously grinning Zeke, grabbing for Boyce's hand and vigorously shaking it. "Welcome to Lincolnton High."

Boyce said nothing as they walked together through the parting, silent crowd. Then, with the other blacks close behind, they continued up the steps to begin their first day of school.

The years passed, and the boys found their way through the first uneasy phases of integration. After graduation, Zeke went to the University of North Carolina, then on to medical school and a residency at the University of Colorado Medical Center.

Boyce became the first Blake to attend college, a source of great pride to his family. After two years at the local community college, he took a job at a Lincolnton paper plant, where he became a supervisor. As time went on, the men each married and completely lost touch.

Then, at the age of twenty-eight, Stoudemire was stricken with bone cancer. His right leg had to be amputated above the knee. Sick from chemotherapy, he lost more than 30 pounds.

Stoudemire now hobbled about on crutches and an artificial leg. He was deeply lonely. "Friends" stopped calling. Neither his work nor his wife's loving support could lift his spirits. All the bright promise of his life seemed to have come to an abrupt end.

Then out of the blue came a phone call.

"Hey, old buddy, we're lookin' for a fourth at bid whiz, and I understand you play a pretty mean game."

Blake's voice was like a tonic. He had heard of his friend's troubles through family, and the two spoke for an hour. Before they hung up, Blake made his old friend promise to "get on the next plane" and fly home.

Now, as his rental car stopped before the Blake cottage, Stoudemire caught sight of Blake at the card table. Boyce looked exactly the way he remembered: muscular, glowing with health and cheer.

Friendship makes prosperity more brilliant, and lightens adversity by dividing and sharing it.

CICERO

6

Stoudemire hesitated. Surely we have nothing in common anymore, he thought. Maybe this visit wasn't such a good idea.

At last he struggled out of the car, propped himself up on his crutches and began to make his way across the lawn.

"Hey, Zeke!" Boyce turned to his friend, his smile as generous as it had always been. "Pull up a chair."

As Zeke settled down, Miss Ruth came out to take away the crutches and set a glass of cold lemonade before him. "You know," she said, putting her hand on his shoulder, "we always used to keep a plate set for you, in case you came around for dinner. Guess I'll get that plate out again. Welcome home, Zeke."

Stoudemire could only manage a nod, tears prickling his eyes.

"Better watch old Zeke there," said Boyce, easing the tension. "Bet he's got a few cards tucked away in that wooden leg of his."

They all laughed. It was good to be home.

During Stoudemire's stay in Lincolnton, his depression began to lift. When he returned to Colorado, he found a new direction for his professional life: the psychiatric care of people suffering devastating illnesses. He accepted a professorship at Duke University in Durham, North Carolina, and he and his wife moved back to the South. Eventually he transferred to Emory University in Atlanta.

He never again lost touch with Blake. They spoke to each other by phone every week and visited often. Over the years, they celebrated the births of Stoudemire's daughter, Anna, and son, Will, and Blake's son, B.J., who joined older sister Vonetta.

One evening in September 1995, Blake found himself limping off the basketball court. When the weakness and pain wouldn't go away, and a local doctor couldn't determine what was wrong, a worried Stoudemire told him to "get on the next flight down here."

At Emory, doctors confirmed Blake had Lou Gehrig's disease, in which the nerves degenerate. It was a death sentence.

Now it was Stoudemire who offered comfort and advice, speaking with Blake almost daily. He helped his friend write a will, and he set up a college fund for B.J. with his own money.

In October 1997 Stoudemire visited his old friend in the hospital. Almost paralyzed, Blake was barely able to raise up his hands to clasp his friend's when he walked into the room. But in his eyes, Stoudemire could still clearly see the spark of Blake's spirit.

"Zeke, there's something I always wanted to tell you," Blake whispered.

Stoudemire leaned in closer.

"You're the lousiest bid whiz player I ever met."

Stoudemire smiled and said he expected that was so.

"That's okay," Boyce reassured him. "I'll still save a space for you at the table up there."

Blake's breath came in shallow gasps as he drifted off to sleep. Stoudemire gently let go of Blake's hands—the hands so often extended to him as a boy, teaching him to fish or defending him against a bully. These were the hands that had reached out to Stoudemire when he'd been crippled in body and spirit.

Well, old friend, we were always there for each other, weren't we? Your hands may have lost their strength, but the strength of our friendship and the memory of your courage will stay with me forever.

Friends are lights in winter; the older the friend, the brighter the light.

ROGER ROSENBLATT

AN UNLIKELY FRIENDSHIP

BY

ALBERT DIBARTOLOMEO

*W*hen the telephone rang that spring evening in 1994, I was in my basement making a jewelry box out of pear wood and listening to Puccini. "It's for you," my wife called.

"Who is it?" I preferred not to be disturbed during those precious moments of self-indulgence.

"A Sister Maria Corona."

I remembered the most recent commentary I had written for the Philadelphia *Inquirer*. "Uh-oh."

The essay had referred to the use of corporal punishment by the nuns of my childhood, and I had used the term "seraphic Frankenstein monster" to describe a fifth-grade sister we kids called Bulldog.

"Could you tell her I'm not in?" I asked my wife.

"I will not. Besides, I already said you were."

My teeth grinding, I uttered a tentative hello. In a friendly voice, the sister introduced herself and said she was calling from Immaculata, a suburb of Philadelphia. Then she got down to business.

"Your commentary was well-written," she said, "but you've done a big disservice to sisters. We already suffer from stereotyping, and your article only furthers that."

"You've taken it too seriously," I said in defense. "Much of it was meant to be humorous."

"Oh, I saw the humor. It's the public that concerns me."

"Well, you could always write a letter to the editor," I suggested.

"I already have."

"Oh."

"Now who was Bulldog?"

The direct question instantly catapulted me back to Saint Gabriel Elementary School, where, in the presence of blue-robed nuns, the notion of evading the truth vanished.

Reluctantly I revealed Bulldog's identity.

"I knew her," the sister told me. "She's buried out here. She was much nicer than you say. I'm sure if you thought about it more, you'd agree with me."

"I'm sure I would." Ashamed of myself for having poked fun at the no-longer-anonymous dead, I was now so uncomfortable that I just wanted to get off the phone. I told the sister that I appreciated her call but that I had to grade a stack of papers.

"Are you a teacher?"

"Yes." I told her that I taught English at a nearby university.

"I was an English teacher too. I've been retired for some time—I'm nearly seventy-nine—but still do teaching."

"Is that so?" I said no more. We soon hung up.

That, I thought, would be the end of Sister Maria Corona. But days later I received a letter from her. Writing in a tiny cursive that forced me to read slowly, she reminded me that sisters were normal women who devoted themselves to God and to doing good.

As a boy, I had experienced their kindness. My family was poor, and, knowing this, parish nuns would periodically summon me to the convent after school. I would stand just inside the vestibule, feeling like an intruder in that serene and dustless place, while a sister retrieved a box of food she had assembled for me.

I returned a letter to Sister Maria Corona explaining my motives for writing the commentary and apologizing, without fully meaning it, for any ill feelings the essay had caused. I sent the letter, certain that my association with the sister had ended.

I received another letter. However, I let it languish in my pile of unanswered mail. In addition to teaching, I had writing to do, books to read, house repairs to make and my wooden boxes to build during that quiet eye in the more blustery winds of my life. Some weeks later those winds became cyclonic.

In June my stepfather became ill, and over the following months I wrote several newspaper commentaries about his experience. After each essay was published, Sister would write, telling me that my stepfather was in her prayers, as was I. I hoped her prayers worked, since I didn't say too many of my own.

My frame of mind then was not much inclined to letter writing, especially to a person who had entered my life as a critic. But I began to answer Sister's letters, more out of politeness than interest.

My stepfather died in October, and the eulogy I wrote was published in the newspaper. Several days later I received a card from Sister along with a pamphlet titled "Dealing With Grief." I didn't feel that I needed the pamphlet. Like my stepfather, I had been taught to be stoical, to absorb the blows that life dealt by "acting like a man." But as Christmas approached, I began to fray.

Despair I had known before, the usual gloomy day or two, but now it mushroomed and began to dominate all my hours. I went to bed with it and rose with it, and it clung to me during the listless days.

At the same time, I felt angry. My stepfather's illness and death, it appeared, had reawakened the hurt caused by the premature death of my natural father. Now their deaths became mixed up together, and so my anguish was doubled.

During this difficult time I wrote a long letter to Sister Maria in which I found myself explaining my state of mind. I speculated about a midlife crisis. I revealed more than I had to anyone but my closest loved ones and dearest friends.

I received a letter from her:

Your beautiful, if poignant, letter touched me deeply. Life holds more valleys than hilltops it seems—yet both have their pain and their promise. It will be my daily prayer that you will soon find peace.

About your dark thoughts, you do realize that is part of the human condition—something we all share. I will always be glad to hear from you, and invite you to come out for a visit any time.

I was not eager to visit. I was afraid that, next to our easy and sincere written exchanges, a face-to-face meeting would be awkward and strained. So I always found reasons for putting it off.

Nevertheless I recognized compassion when I saw it. Sister wrote:

I have had periods of emotional turmoil, too, at times quite bad. Perhaps that is why I empathize with your feelings.

I like the definition of a friend: one to whom you can pour it all out—wheat and chaff together—knowing that he/she will listen, take out that which is important and throw the rest away. It would be so good to meet and really cement this friendship that I think was a gift from God.

I didn't know about divine presents, but I had begun to care about the nun's welfare, as she seemed to care about mine. We appeared sometimes to be in coincident states, although it was her body, not mind, that gave her trouble. She wrote me several letters from the hospital where she was being cared for, as she put it, "another heart scare." She also sent the rosary she had been using in the hospital. I had not prayed the rosary since the sixth grade, but I was touched that she parted with that particular one.

While Sister Maria recuperated, I began to suffer insomnia. The nights seemed endless, the clock frozen between three and four in the morning. I tried to read. I watched television. I paced the quiet house or sat still in my study, listening to the groaning of the dead tree in our neighbor's yard as it moved with the wind. I even made wooden boxes—all in an effort to tire myself enough to sleep. But sleep refused to come.

After the third or fourth night like that in a row, I took the rosary from my bureau, and I prayed. I hung it around my neck when I worked on my midnight boxes, and I carried it in my pocket when I left the house.

The rosary helped, but my bloodshot and circled eyes told me that I needed professional attention. I made the necessary call.

After I told Sister Maria of my decision, she wrote:

I'm happy to hear that you're going to enter therapy. Don't be afraid of medication. It helped me over the humps. Each letter you send reveals a loss of fear in opening up to someone who, even a Sister stranger, has you on her mind often and in her prayers always. Yesterday I learned I may need a new knee. This getting old is definitely not for sissies!

She was far from that. I admired her for her courage and spirit in the face of her physical troubles. Life dealt out its knocks, she believed,

No man is useless while he has a friend.

ROBERT LOUIS STEVENSON

14

but it was ultimately good. Sister Maria suffered with grace. I could not help but be impressed.

In the spring, soon after my depression began to lift, I decided that I wanted to meet this woman.

"Your letter was a joy to my heart," she replied. "I look forward to our meeting. My bionic knee is doing well."

After more than a year of corresponding, I met Sister Maria on a Tuesday in mid-August at Villa Maria by the Sea in Stone Harbor, New Jersey, the vacation home for her order, Sisters Servants of the Immaculate Heart of Mary. "So, we meet at last," Sister Maria Corona said, smiling broadly.

"Yes," I said, taking her outstretched hand. In the other she held a cane. She wore bifocals, and a rim of steel-gray hair peeked from beneath her veil. She looked younger than I had expected. Her bright eyes were intelligent, kind and welcoming. They glinted with humor too. After we exchanged pleasantries, she suggested that we walk to the ocean.

Sister Maria held on to my arm now and then to keep herself steady. I offered her my hand when we stepped from the curb.

Soon we stood gazing at the sun worshipers and children bobbing and squealing in the swells and the in-rushing surf. I smiled at the sight.

"Look at it," she said, gesturing to what she called the "majestic mystery" of the sea. "It's all surface to our eyes now. But beneath it are great depths and life of all kinds. That's what people are when we first meet them. But we only have to go below the surface a bit to see one another's hearts."

I nodded. "Our letters."

"Yes."

When she first began to write, Sister must have intuited that I was troubled and lost, adrift on seas I could only pretend to navigate. I was grateful that she had thrown me a line with her letters.

When we returned to Villa Maria and sat facing the ocean, I gave her a small gift I had made during those anguished days of my depression—a box of tiger-stripe maple with a lid of figured walnut. In it I had placed an ample supply of postage stamps. I wanted her to keep writing. I needed to hear from my friend.

"It's beautiful," she said, "a very thoughtful present. Thank you so much."

She held the box in her lap as we talked into the lengthening afternoon. As the hours slid by, I came to know Sister even better. She shared her memories of a trip on a banana boat to Peru, where she had done missionary work. She told of her work at 13 schools during her teaching career.

I soon recognized that she and the other women who had chosen the convent over a more conventional life were far more complex than I had allowed myself to believe. What Sister Maria gave me that day was a moment of insight, a gift far greater than the wooden box I had brought her.

As she walked me to the door, we passed the chapel, now nearly full with nuns who had gathered for evening prayers. We embraced as we said good-bye.

Outside the sun was still bright. Before I had gone ten steps, the voices from the chapel lifted in song. I paused and allowed the sweet, angelic voices to wash over me.

Although her infirmities have since caused her to live in a nursing home at the age of eighty-three, Sister Maria Corona is clear of head. She still teaches part time. She continues to write, and like sunshine and salt breezes on a summer's day by the sea, her words still nourish my soul.

Wishing to be friends is quick work, but

friendship is a slow-ripening fruit.

ARISTOTLE

WISDOM OF
BEAR WOOD

BY
MICHAEL WELZENBACH

When I was twelve years old, my family moved to England, the fourth major move in my short life. My father's government job demanded that he go overseas every few years, so I was used to wrenching myself away from friends.

We rented a sprawling eighteenth-century farmhouse in Berkshire. Nearby were ancient castles and venerable churches. Loving nature, however, I was most delighted by the endless patchwork of farms and woodland that surrounded our house. In the deep woods that verged against our back fence, a network of paths led almost everywhere, and pheasants rocketed off into the dense laurels and bracken ahead as you walked.

I spent most of my time roaming the woods and fields alone, playing at Robin Hood, daydreaming, collecting bugs and bird-watching. It was heaven for a boy—but a lonely heaven. Keeping to myself was my way of not forming attachments that I would only have to abandon the next time we moved. But one day I became attached through no design of my own.

We had been in England about six months when old farmer Crawford gave me permission to roam about his immense property. I started hiking there every weekend, up a long, sloping hill to an almost impenetrable stand of trees called Bear Wood. It was my secret fortress, almost a holy place, I thought. Slipping through a barbed-wire fence, I'd leave the bright sun and the twitter and rustle of insects and animals outside and creep into another world—a vaulted cathedral, with tree trunks for pillars and eons' accumulation of long brown needles for a softly carpeted floor. My own breathing rang in my ears, and the slightest stirring of any woodland creature echoed through this private paradise.

One spring afternoon I wandered near where I thought I'd glimpsed a pond the week before. I proceeded quietly, careful not to alarm a jay or magpie that might loudly warn other creatures to hide.

Perhaps this is why the frail old lady I nearly ran into was as startled as I was. She caught her breath, instinctively touching her throat with her hand. Then, recovering quickly, she gave a welcoming smile that instantly put me at ease. A pair of powerful-looking binoculars dangled from her neck. "Hello, young man," she said. "Are you American or Canadian?"

American, I explained in a rush, and I lived over the hill, and I was just seeing if there was a pond, and farmer Crawford had said it was okay, and anyhow, I was on my way home, so good-bye.

As I started to turn, the woman smiled and asked, "Did you see the little owl from the spinney over there today?" She pointed toward the edge of the wood.

She knew about the owls? I was amazed. According to some unkind schoolmates, only "twitchers" (British slang for bird-watchers) like me knew anything about birds. Normal kids used slingshots.

"No," I replied, "but I've seen them before. Never close though. They always see me first."

The woman laughed. "Yes, they're wary," she said. "But then, game-keepers have been shooting them ever since they got here. They're introduced, you know, not native."

"They're not?" I asked, fascinated. Anybody who knew this sort of stuff was definitely cool—even if she was trespassing in my special place.

"Oh, no!" she answered, laughing again. "At home I have books on birds that explain all about them. In fact," she said suddenly, "I was about to go back for tea and jam tart. Would you care to join me?"

I had been warned against going off with strangers, but somehow I sensed the old woman was harmless. "Sure," I said.

"I'm Mrs. Robertson-Glasgow," she introduced herself, extending a fine, transparent hand.

"Michael," I said, taking it clumsily in my own.

We set off, the old woman striding along at a surprisingly brisk clip. She told me how she and her husband had moved to Berkshire after he'd retired as a college professor about ten years earlier. "He passed away last year," she said, looking suddenly wistful. "So now I'm alone, and I have all this time to walk the fields."

Soon I saw a small brick cottage that glowed pinkly in the westering sun. Mrs. Robertson-Glasgow opened the door and invited me in. I gazed about in silent admiration at the jumble of bookshelves, glass-fronted cases containing figures of ivory, ebony and carved stone, and cabinets full of fossils. There were glass terraria writhing with mosses and ferns, trays of pinned butterflies and, best of all, a dozen or so stuffed birds—including a slightly moth-eaten, glass-eyed eagle owl, tilting on its wire perch.

"Wow!" was all I could say.

"Does your mother expect you home at a particular time?" she asked as she ran the water for tea.

"No," I lied. Then, glancing at the clock, I added, "Well, maybe by five." That gave me almost an hour, not nearly enough time to ask about every single object in the room. Between mouthfuls of tea and jam tart I learned all sorts of things—how to find fossilized sand dollars in the pebbles along the public footpaths; or that you could tell if dormice were about by the way they chiseled into hazelnuts.

The hour went by much too swiftly. Mrs. Robertson-Glasgow had to practically push me out the door. But she sent me home with two large tomes, one full of glorious illustrations of birds, and one of butterflies and other insects. I promised to return them the next weekend if she didn't mind my coming by. She smiled and said she'd look forward to that.

I had made the best friend in the world.

When I returned the books, she lent me more. Soon I began to see her almost every weekend, and my well of knowledge about natural history began to brim over. At school, I earned the nickname "Prof" and some respect from my fellow students. Even the school bully brought me a dead water rail he had found (or more likely shot), to identify.

During the summer I spent blissfully long days with my friend. I discovered she made the finest shortbread in the universe. We would explore Bear Wood, munching happily and discussing the books she had lent me. In the afternoons we would retire to the cottage, and she would talk about her husband—what a fine man he'd been. Once or twice she seemed about to cry and left the room quickly to make more tea. But she always came back smiling.

As time passed, I did not notice that she was growing frailer and less inclined to laugh. Familiarity sometimes renders people physically invisible, for you find yourself talking to the heart—to the essence, as it were, rather than to the face. I suspected, of course, that she was lonely; I did not know she was ill.

Back at school, I began to grow quickly. I played soccer and made a good friend. But I still stopped by the cottage on weekends, and there was always fresh shortbread.

One morning when I went downstairs to the kitchen, there was a familiar-looking biscuit tin on the table. I eyed it as I went to the refrigerator.

My mother was regarding me with a strange gentleness. "Son," she began, painfully. And from the tone of her voice I knew everything instantly.

She rested her hand on the biscuit tin. "Mr. Crawford brought these by this morning." She paused, and I could tell she was having difficulty. "Mrs. Robertson-Glasgow left them for you."

I stared out the window, tears stinging my eyes.

"I'm sorry, Michael, but she died yesterday," she went on. "She was very old and very ill, and it was time."

My mother put her arm about my shoulder. "You made her very happy, because she was lonely," she said. "You were lucky to be such a good friend for her."

Wordlessly, I took the tin to my room and set it on my bed. Then, hurrying downstairs, I burst through the front door and ran to the woods.

I wandered for a long time, until my eyes had dried and I could see clearly again. It was spring—almost exactly a year since I'd met the old woman in Bear Wood. I looked around me and realized how much I now knew. I knew where to look for bee orchids in the long grass. I knew to look for water striders, whirligig beetles and dragonfly larvae in a

A friend hears the song in my heart and sings it to me when my memory fails.

PIONEER GIRLS
LEADERS' HANDBOOK

long-abandoned horse trough. And I knew that back in my bedroom I had a tin of the best shortbread in the universe, and I should go and eat it, savoring every crumb. And that's just what I did.

In time, that old round tin filled up with dried leaves, fossils and bits of colorful stone, a dead stag beetle, a flint arrowhead and countless other odds and ends. I still have it.

But I have much more, the legacy of that long-ago encounter in Bear Wood. It is a wisdom tutored by nature itself, about the seen and the unseen, about things that change and things that are changeless, and about the fact that, no matter how seemingly disparate two souls may be, they possess the potential for that most precious, rare thing—an enduring and rewarding friendship.

THE SEARCH FOR BILLY

❧

BY

DAVID REED

In war-ravaged South Korea in 1952, more than 100,000 orphans roamed the countryside. One of them was twelve-year-old Baik Sung-Hak. Dressed in rags, he subsisted on the garbage that was discarded by American soldiers.

Then a U.S. artillery unit took him in as a "washy-washy boy." A half-dozen such youngsters did laundry, cleaned latrines and ran errands. The youngest and smallest, Baik got no pay, but the soldiers gave him food, candy and gum.

Among the GIs was Billy, a twenty-year-old private first class. Shy and gentle, he never swore or raised his voice. He always had an air of sadness. He, too, was an orphan, he said.

Billy looked upon Baik as a younger brother, and built a bed for him in one of the bunkers. When a new commander ordered the washy-washy boys out of the bunkers, Billy and Baik moved air mattresses and blankets into a half-track, a truck-size armored vehicle.

Over and over, Billy told the boy he should always behave decently and be honest with others. Billy was distressed whenever he heard Baik use a four-letter word. "Don't talk that way," he would say. "It ain't right."

Over and over Billy told the boy he should always behave decently and be honest

Billy taught Baik some English. He had him recite: "This is candy. This is a machine gun." The boy could never say machine gun; it always came out "sheengun."

Day and night, Billy loaded 105-mm. howitzers that pounded enemy positions. Baik brought Billy coffee. Whenever the GI was late returning to the half-track, Baik feared that he had been killed.

Now and then the boy's nerves cracked, and he would weep uncontrollably. Billy would put his arm around him and say, "Don't worry. The war won't last forever."

One day, while Baik was standing on a riverbank, an enemy shell landed on a fuel drum. Drenched with burning gasoline, Baik leaped into the water. Billy came running and carried him to a jeep, which rushed him to an aid station.

It was 18 hours before Baik regained consciousness. He was swathed in bandages—the front of his body had been burned from head to toe.

Some time later Baik opened his eyes to find Billy's sad face looking down at him. "Don't worry," Billy said. "You're going to get well." After three months, Baik recovered sufficiently to return to the unit. Near Christmas, Billy gave the boy a box.

"What's this?" Baik asked.

"Open it and see," Billy replied.

The boy was staggered. Inside the box were blue jeans, shirts, shoes and a pair of lined boots. Until then, Baik had worn hopelessly large Army uniforms. Billy had written someone in the States—Baik thought it was a sister—requesting the clothing.

The boy's world was shattered a few days later when all washy-washy boys under fifteen were sent to orphanages. Packed off to Seoul, Baik soon escaped. He tried to return to Billy's unit, but military police sent him away.

Baik learned of a U.S. medical facility at Sokcho, where he got a janitorial job. The staff there continued to treat his burns.

25

At age fourteen, fully recovered and with the war over, Baik headed for Seoul. He worked up to 18 hours a day as a janitor in a factory that produced caps for schoolboys. Bright and eager, he attracted the attention of the owner. By eighteen, Baik was managing two stores and a small factory.

Soon after his nineteenth birthday, Baik quit his job and rented a tiny store. Each evening he worked past midnight making hats. At dawn he would go to the market to buy more material. And all day long, he waited on customers. After six months, he hired an assistant. Six months later, he took on a second.

Today Baik is one of the richest men in Korea. He employs 3800 people in 19 plants in five countries, including the United States. The factories grossed $85 million in 1989, turning out plastics, corrugated boxes and 48 million baseball caps, including more than half of all those sold in the United States.

Through the years, convinced that his success in life was due to the strong moral example provided by Billy, Baik yearned to see him again. But how?

In the mid-1980s, as a monument to Billy, Baik bought 45 acres near the place where he and his friend had met. There he built a $5-million village that today houses 600 orphans and elderly, handicapped and once destitute people. The village also includes a church, a clinic, a job-training center and its own farm. Baik named the home for the handicapped "Billy's House."

When I first met Baik in Seoul four years ago, he said, "Someday, somehow, I will find Billy."

Baik recalled that Billy's unit had a bucking bronco as a symbol. I learned that it was the emblem of the 300th Armored Field Artillery Battalion, part of the Wyoming National Guard.

An article I wrote for a national magazine asked anyone with information about Billy to contact the magazine. Although more than 300 readers responded, none of the leads panned out.

The search for Billy became a job for a professional. Mutual friends introduced me to Courtland Jones, nearly seventy, a soft-spoken resident of Vienna, Virginia, who had spent most of his career smoking out Soviet-bloc spies. He was deeply moved by Baik's story.

The first break came in a letter from Robert G. Davis of Colorado Springs, the long-retired first sergeant of the 300th's Battery A. He did not remember Billy, but had a snapshot of four washy-washy boys. The smallest of them was swathed in bandages from his neck to his waist.

Baik met Courtland Jones in New York City. Shown the photo, Baik was sure he was that bandaged boy.

Thus, the search for Billy was narrowed to Battery A. But as many as 130 men were in the battery at any one time, and during the war several hundred men had rotated through it.

Jones flew to Cheyenne, hoping to find Billy among veterans of the Wyoming National Guard. An officer explained that because the 300th had been federalized when sent to Korea, the original guardsmen who rotated home were replaced by regular Army personnel. By the time Baik met Billy, a member of the 300th could have come from anywhere in the United States.

Working from a 1952 roster, Jones found 12 men named Billy or some variant. He tracked down nine by telephone. None was Baik's benefactor.

Jones next met with a Battery A corporal named Wayne Secord, who now lives in Enola, Pennsylvania. Although Secord did not recall Billy, he remembered Baik as the smallest washy-washy boy. Secord then handed Jones a photo of himself and four Battery A buddies. The names were written on the back—Sergeants Sabatino and Wise, Corporal Haak and Private first class D. Beattie.

Jones looked at the photo and thought it was useless. He had no way of knowing that one of the four named was Billy.

All other leads went nowhere. Reluctantly, after a year of searching for him, Jones closed the file on Billy.

Toward the end of 1988, retired first-sergeant Davis had an inspiration. He convened a reunion in Kansas City, Missouri, for those Battery A vets he and Jones had located. He asked them to bring their war photos.

Fourteen men who had not seen one another for more than 35 years showed up. Baik flew in from Seoul. For three days, he studied more than a thousand faded snapshots. As he was looking at one of them on the last day of the reunion, he suddenly shouted, "That's Billy!"

There was no name on the photo, taken by LaVern Babel, now a farmer in Lindsay, Nebraska. The men racked their brains. Then someone said, "That's Dave Beattie!"

Davis checked the roster and found the name David Beattie, serial number RA13283670. Baik, with his poor English, had confused "Billy" for "Beattie."

Courtland Jones, on the case again, found that a David Beattie with that serial number had enlisted in the Army in Philadelphia in 1948. The telephone directory and motor-vehicle files didn't help. Burrowing through other records, Jones learned of a David Beattie in Port Richmond, a working-class neighborhood in Philadelphia. Jones and I decided to call on this David Beattie at his home, a narrow three-story row house across the street from a paint factory.

A man with a thick shock of gray hair answered our knock. Yes, he said, he had fought in Korea. Yes, he remembered befriending a little boy. Was the youngster ever involved in an accident, we inquired. "Yes," answered Beattie. "He got burned."

If you want an accounting

of your worth,

count your friends.

MERRY BROWNE

A small smile crossed Courtland Jones's face. *After nearly three years,* he thought, *we've finally got our man.*

Beattie, now fifty-eight, was just as Baik remembered him—humble and quiet. He radiated a basic decency. When told of Baik's gratitude, Beattie looked perplexed and said, "I don't know why he's making such a big deal about this. I'd have done that for anyone."

Born in Philadelphia, Beattie had grown up in foster homes. His first foster mother, Mary Poole, had up to ten boys at a time. She drilled it into the boys that they should always tell the truth and work diligently. Each Sunday she marched her charges off to church.

When Beattie was fourteen, Mary Poole could no longer care for her foster children. Welfare officials placed the heartbroken boy in the home of Cathy Crida, for whom Beattie developed a strong affection. He stayed three years, until she, too, could no longer look after him. With no place else to go, he joined the Army at seventeen. The box of Christmas clothing had been sent not by a sister, as Baik thought, but by Cathy Crida.

Discharged as a private first class in 1957, Beattie worked for the next 20 years in a bakery, loading trucks. At the time the bakery shut down in 1978, he was married and had young children. He went on to eke out a living by working temporary jobs.

In 1982 Beattie finally was hired as a night janitor in downtown Philadelphia. He has kept the job and today earns $8 an hour operating a freight elevator and manhandling drums of trash onto the loading dock.

Beattie counts himself a lucky man. In good health, he and his wife, Dorothy, have four children and a happy marriage.

A sports fan, Beattie often attends untelevised Phillies games on weekends. What he could not know, all through the years, was that many of the baseball caps sold at the park were manufactured by the Korean urchin he had befriended many years before.

After talking with Beattie, I telephoned Baik. "We've found Billy," I told him.

Three hours later, Baik was on a 16-hour flight to Philadelphia. The next morning, we set out for Beattie's home.

"I'm nervous," Baik said. He waited in the car while I went into Beattie's house.

"He's outside," I said to Dave Beattie.

"What'll I call him?" Beattie asked apprehensively. "Should I call him Mister?"

"Call him what you used to call him—Hak," I said.

Beattie stepped out into the sunlit street. Baik came toward him. They gazed at each other, then solemnly shook hands.

Beattie smiled and said, "You got big since I last saw you, Hak."

Baik smiled back. "You got a lot of gray hair."

For six emotionally draining hours, the multimillionaire and the night-shift janitor sat at Beattie's kitchen table and talked about the war, the men of Battery A, their jobs, their families, their dreams. In Baik's desire to repay those long-ago kindnesses, he found there was nothing Beattie really needed or wanted. The house was almost paid for. Beattie had never owned a car and didn't want one; he traveled on buses and trolleys.

Still, Baik continued to look for a way to be of financial assistance—perhaps by helping Beattie's daughter Dorothy, twenty-three, to study nursing, and a son, Tommy, eighteen, to go to college.

It was a generous gesture. But the real meaning of this reunion is that common decency—spun by two loving foster mothers and woven into the threadbare life of a Korean boy by an ordinary GI, and later by the boy into the lives of hundreds of unfortunate people—is its own reward.

A friend may well be reckoned the

masterpiece of Nature.

RALPH WALDO EMERSON

IT WAS A GOOD BARN

BY

EDWARD ZIEGLER

An old friendship had grown cold. Where once there had been closeness, there was only strain. Now pride kept me from picking up the phone.

Then one day I dropped in on another old friend, who's had a long career as a minister and counselor. We were seated in his study—surrounded by maybe a thousand books—and fell into deep conversation about everything from small computers to the tormented life of Beethoven.

The subject finally turned to friendship and how perishable it seems to be these days. I mentioned my own experience as an example. "Relationships are mysteries," my friend said. "Some endure. Others fall apart."

Gazing out his window to the wooded Vermont hills, he pointed toward a neighboring farm. "Used to be a large barn over there." Next to a red-frame house were the footings of what had been a sizable structure.

"It was solidly built, probably in the 1870s. But like so many of the places around here, it went down because people left for richer lands in the

Midwest. No one took care of the barn. Its roof needed patching; rainwater got under the eaves and dripped down inside the posts and beams."

One day a high wind came along, and the whole barn began to tremble. "You could hear this creaking, first, like old sailing-ship timbers, and then a sharp series of cracks and a tremendous roaring sound. Suddenly it was a heap of scrap lumber.

"After the storm blew over, I went down and saw these beautiful, old oak timbers, solid as could be. I asked the fellow who owns the place what had happened. He said he figured the rainwater had settled in the pinholes, where wooden dowels held the joints together. Once those pins were rotted, there was nothing to link the giant beams together."

We both gazed down the hill. Now all that was left of the barn was its cellar hole and its border of lilac shrubs.

My friend said he had turned the incident over and over in his mind, and finally came to recognize some parallels between building a barn and building a friendship: no matter how strong you are, how notable your attainments, you have enduring significance only in your relationship to others.

"To make your life a sound structure that will serve others and fulfill your own potential," he said, "you have to remember that strength, however massive, can't endure unless it has the interlocking support of others. Go it alone and you'll inevitably tumble.

"Relationships have to be cared for," he added, "like the roof of a barn. Letters unwritten, thanks unsaid, confidences violated, quarrels unsettled—all these act like rainwater seeping into the pegs, weakening the link between the beams."

My friend shook his head. "It was a good barn. And it would have taken very little to keep it in good repair. Now it will probably never be rebuilt."

Later that afternoon I got ready to leave. "You wouldn't like to borrow my phone to make a call, I don't suppose?" he asked.

"Yes," I said, "I think I would. Very much."

ORDEAL ON KILLINGTON PEAK

BY

JON VARA

erard Healy and Mark Molz lifted their blue, white and gold Piper Arrow off the runway at Montpelier, Vermont, on a gray afternoon in January 1991, expecting an uneventful flight to the South Jersey Regional Airport. Healy, a thirty-nine-year-old flight instructor, and Molz, a thirty-five-year-old student pilot and lawyer, were returning home from a training flight.

Suddenly, cruising at their assigned altitude of 8000 feet, the aircraft entered a bank of clouds, and a glaze of freezing rain began to accumulate on the windshield.

Immediately realizing the peril they now faced, Healy radioed air-traffic controllers in the FAA's Boston Center, which handles aircraft in a large sector of New England.

"Boston, this is November Seven Seven Seven Charlie Lima. We're picking up some ice here. Could we possibly have a higher altitude?"

Icing conditions can change at different altitudes, Healy knew. By climbing, he hoped to fly out of his present danger.

"Okay, Triple Seven Charlie Lima, you're clear to climb to and maintain one zero thousand," a controller directed.

At 8500 feet, the clouds began to thin and the sky grew brighter. A few hundred feet more—another minute at their rate of climb—would put them safely in the clear, Healy thought.

Then, unexpectedly, a hydraulic pump hummed to life beneath the cabin, and the yellow GEAR IN TRANSIT light blinked on. Both men heard and felt the distinctive clunk of the landing gear unfolding from its housing.

Molz, looking out the left window, could see that the wing-mounted pitot tube was completely covered with ice. Air flows through the tube in flight to measure a plane's airspeed. With Charlie Lima's pitot blocked by ice, the sensor had interpreted the reduced airflow as a decrease in speed and, as the aircraft is engineered to do, had automatically lowered the gear in preparation for landing.

Healy realized that he and Molz were now in even bigger trouble.

The Piper Arrow was already climbing in a nose-up attitude, and the sudden increased drag of the lowered gear shoved the nose up still farther, slowing the plane still more. To prevent the aircraft from stalling out of control, Healy threw it into a steep diving turn to pick up airspeed, as Molz tried to retract the landing gear manually. Healy realized that if Molz was unsuccessful, the Piper Arrow was going nowhere except down. At 1:30 P.M., he informed Boston Center that they were unable to climb and asked to be assigned a lower altitude.

"Okay, Triple Seven Charlie Lima," the controller replied, "descend and maintain 7000."

Ninety-five seconds passed. Then Healy radioed again.

"Boston, seven's no good for us either. We're really picking up ice now."

The thickest ice forms on the leading edges of a plane's wings, changing their aerodynamic shape and robbing them of lift. Ice also forms on a plane's propeller, leading to lowered thrust and decreased airspeed, which can reduce lift even more. A plane that ices up beyond a certain critical point simply falls out of the sky.

For the next 11 minutes, Triple Seven Charlie Lima drew closer and closer to that point as Healy, with Molz's help and guidance from Boston Center, struggled to reach Rutland State Airport, a few miles to the southwest. But ice on the radio antennas distorted voice communications and made it impossible for Healy to receive the signals from the airport's navigation beacon.

At 1:43 Boston Center asked, "November Triple Seven Charlie Lima, what is your present altitude?"

"I'm at five point five [5500], Boston."

"Triple Seven Charlie Lima, are you able to maintain at least five point five or climb to six thousand?" the Boston Center controller asked.

"Negative. I'm down to four point two now—"

At that moment, through a narrow, ice-free strip at the bottom of the left window, Molz saw a tree-covered ridge materialize from out of the clouds.

"Pull up!" he yelled, instinctively yanking back on Charlie Lima's controls.

"We're gonna stall!" Healy shouted. He shoved the controls forward as the plane skimmed over the 4241-foot summit of Vermont's Killington Peak. It shot through a swirl of clouds over the ridge, then slammed into snow-shrouded pines at 70 miles per hour.

The trees, brittle from a week-long spell of below-freezing temperatures, split and shattered. Charlie Lima's left wing sheared from the fuselage and hung in the branches as the rest of the plane half-turned and plunged to earth.

At 1:44 Boston Center called: "Triple Seven Charlie Lima, what are your flight conditions now?"

There was no answer.

The Piper Arrow's last-known position was roughly a mile and a half northeast of Rutland State Airport. Private and commercial aircraft overflying the area were immediately asked to listen for the downed plane's ELT—emergency locator transmitter. This device sends signals on radio frequency 121.5. No transmission was reported, however.

The first volunteer Civil Air Patrol search-and-rescue flight, piloted by Tim Maxfield, a Rutland businessman, and Robin Guarino, an engineer, took off from Rutland around 4:00 P.M. They had 60 square miles of heavily wooded terrain to cover in less than two hours of daylight. The search was akin to looking for nail clippers in an acre of ankle-high grass.

Combing the area, Maxfield and Guarino saw nothing, heard nothing. At about six o'clock they made a final, slow pass around Killington Peak and returned to the airport.

A second CAP aircraft, flown by commercial pilot Mike Tassielli, took off from Burlington to search at a higher altitude, hoping to pick up the downed plane's ELT. Several times Tassielli detected a peculiar clicking sound on the 121.5 frequency. The transmission, however—if that's what it was—was weak and intermittent. By 11:00 P.M., Tassielli had also discontinued the search.

Triple Seven Charlie Lima had come to rest on its right side, with its only exit blocked by the twisted right wing. Burning gasoline was pouring from ruptured fuel lines. Molz reached across the cabin, exposing his right side to the full force of the flames boiling up between the seats, and grappled frantically for the door latches. It was like being in a gas grill. He could feel his skin sizzling.

"Mark!" Healy yelled. "Brace yourself against me, and kick out your window." If they were to survive, Healy realized, they would have to be a team, work together. Neither would get out alone.

Molz put his back against Healy's, kicked out the window and dived out. Healy scrambled after him. Fearing an explosion, the two backed away from the 20-foot flames.

Healy's right wrist had been broken in two places on impact. His pants and boots were covered with melted plastic, and his hands and ears had suffered severe burns. But two sweatshirts and quilted thermal-underwear bottoms had shielded him from the worst flames.

The best mirror is a friend's eye.

GAELIC PROVERB

Molz had not been as lucky. Protected only by a T-shirt now burned to a rag, his upper body, arms and face bore extensive second- and third-degree burns. One moccasin had come off during the scramble from the plane, and on his left foot he now wore only a thin cotton sock. He was bleeding heavily from two deep gashes on his forehead.

The plane's tail section had broken off from the rest of the fuselage. As the flames died, Molz crawled into it for shelter from the wind and cold. Healy gathered wood and piled it around a still-burning tire in an effort to provide some warmth. He stripped off his outer, hooded sweatshirt and gave it to the already freezing Molz.

Healy also checked on the ELT, which was clipped to a bracket at the far end of the tail section. His heart sank when he saw the device had been badly damaged. Improvising, he was able, after about an hour, to jury-rig it and click out an SOS.

Together the two men operated the ELT for a couple of hours, uncertain whether its signals were being sent. Their hopes soared when they heard the hum of an aircraft nearby, but it soon flew off.

It was dark now, and stars twinkled through the treetops. Cold had become their main enemy. Gusts of wind shook the fuselage. Temperatures at the mountain's summit would surely drop to zero or less.

They lay huddled together in the narrow tail section. Everything they might have used for warmth—fiberglass insulation, foam from the seats—had gone up in flames. Both men were wet: Healy from snow, Molz from the plasma that leaked from the fist-size burn blisters on his arms, back, neck and hands.

They helped each other however they could. To keep awake, they prayed, sang and talked—about their families, their accomplishments, everything. Healy's head was bare, and Molz wrapped his arms around it to retain heat. As the temperature dropped, Molz's left foot started to go numb; Healy warmed it between his legs.

It was no use. Long before dawn, both of Molz's feet were frozen, and Healy knew that his own feet were becoming frostbitten. As the cold tightened its grip, both men began having muscle spasms. Neither could dismiss the thought that they might now perish.

Finally morning came. The sky was clear, and they soon heard search planes. Healy tore a scrap of sheet aluminum from the fuselage and polished it on his pants, expecting to use it as a signal mirror.

But by midmorning, clouds had begun to close in again and the search planes disappeared. The evening before, the two men had talked of trying to walk out, and now they spoke of it again. But Molz couldn't even stand. He urged Healy to go for help on his own while he was still able to move. Healy rejected the idea. Their chances were better if they stuck together.

Healy began preparing for another night. He collected evergreen branches and placed them in the tail section for insulation. He packed up snow at the opening to cut the wind. And he did one other thing.

Every few minutes, he paused, knee-deep in the snow, stood erect, cupped his blistered hands around his mouth and called out over the quiet hillside.

"Help! Help!"

Molz watched skeptically as Healy shouted at the empty forest. *He's a dummy,* Molz thought. *No one will ever hear him.*

"Help! Help!"

Fred Mallett and Scott Freundlich, both from New York, were on a little-used trail down Killington, a popular ski area. They had been on the slopes all weekend, and this was to be their last run of the day. Just then, momentarily stopped a couple of miles from the summit, they heard a faint call for help from the thick woods to their right.

The two skiers were perplexed to hear a voice in such a remote location. It was difficult to imagine another skier venturing so far from the trail, and they could think of no other reason for anyone to be there. Mallett and Freundlich skied a few hundred yards farther down the slope to a more promising spot for heading off the trail.

They asked the next skier who came by to alert the ski patrol that someone seemed to be in trouble. Then, leaving their skis by the trail as markers, they trudged into the woods, calling out, "Where are you?"

The snow was hip-high in places, and their rigid plastic ski boots made it difficult for them to keep their footing. They kept hearing "This way, this way," and they'd answer back, "Keep yelling, we're coming."

After three-quarters of an hour Freundlich and Mallett stood at the base of a steep ridge below where Healy and Molz had struggled from the crash almost 24 hours earlier.

"Look for the wing up in the tree," the downed fliers shouted. Mallett and Freundlich finally saw the wing and worked their way up to it. There they found Healy and Molz, still huddled together. The two men, using the buddy system, watching out for each other, encouraging each other, had survived their terrible ordeal.

The skiers gave Molz and Healy their jackets, hats and gloves. Half an hour later, other rescuers arrived. By midafternoon the fliers were at Rutland Regional Medical Center.

Gerard Healy's burns and fractured wrist healed quickly, but his frostbitten feet troubled him for the rest of the winter. Molz spent four weeks in the hospital. His burns required extensive treatment, and although doctors feared that he might lose his severely frostbitten left foot, he didn't. By late spring he had logged enough flight time to pass the exam for a private pilot's license.

Looking back, Molz says his survival was like being born again. "When I knew we were safe," he says, "I lay there and I cried."

But what both Molz and Healy most remember is that they survived together. "If either of us had been alone, he never would have made it."

Love is like the wild rose-briar;

Friendship like the holly-tree.

The holly is dark when the rose-briar blooms,

But which will bloom most constantly?

EMILY BRONTË

All at
once we
realized
why
hadn't
spoken to
before
Talking
was hard
for her

FRIENDS OF THE ROAD

BY

KIM SHIPPEY

*M*y wife and I used to feel that it was virtually impossible to be a true friend to someone whose name we didn't know. How wrong we were! Years of Sunday-morning bus trips through the city with the same group of "nameless" people have radically changed our thinking.

On our way to church, we gather at the bus station in the early hours, in rain, snow and in steamy midsummer. In these circumstances, teamwork is far more important than knowing names.

Someone makes sure that our regular driver is on duty and checks that he has punched up the right destination on the front of the bus. His walrus mustache, snowy at the edges, stands out in rich contrast to his well-worn face. He smiles benignly at each passenger, expecting him or her to put the correct change in the box, and to obey the written and unwritten rules that govern each trip.

There's definitely no smoking on his bus, no littering, no rudeness, and few strident bells to signal stops. He makes it his business to learn the stop of every regular passenger.

Before we take off, we all participate in a mental roll call: Where's the silent woman who sits up front and never responds to our cheery greetings? Here she comes. Her worn clothing suggests she doesn't have much money to spare, but she always clutches an extra cup of coffee for the driver.

Where's the factory security guard who comes off a long night shift and somehow makes us feel protected? There he is, slumping in his seat with his eyes closed until the precise moment that the driver approaches his corner. Then, reluctantly, his eyes open, and he heaves himself to the front door of the bus.

There's the rotund fellow who comes into town, buys his Sunday newspaper, joins us for a bagel in the coffee shop, and rides back to his stop with his paper clutched under his arm. One morning, as he moved forward to board, he collapsed on the sidewalk. We all leaped to his aid. Anonymous arms cradled his head until an ambulance arrived. A prayerful silence reigned as we pulled away. Then someone spotted his newspaper in the gutter, and the driver stopped while we slipped the paper into the ambulance beside its passenger. The bus was very late that morning.

The next Sunday the man was back with a fresh newspaper and an unmistakably grateful smile.

We also get smiles from a Mexican couple as they board the bus hand in hand. When they alight, they're still holding hands. The woman was pregnant late last year, and one day her change of shape confirmed that she'd delivered the child. We even felt a little pride at the thought of our extended family.

A group of Haitians make a tricky connection with us 15 blocks from the station. Their cross-town bus invariably arrives at the changeover point later than we do. But our Haitian friends have such a sense of fun—even early on Sunday morning—that we hate to leave the meeting point without them. When they're all aboard, we chuckle and nod. Who needs words—or names—when you can speak from the heart?

For many months, our only sadness lay in our inability to establish the same rapport with the silent woman at the front of the bus. Then, one evening, we went to a fish restaurant located on our bus route. We were shown to a table alongside someone sitting alone, huddled in an overcoat that we recognized before we saw the owner's face. It was the woman from the bus.

We greeted her with the friendly familiarity we'd shown all year, but this time—like ice floes unlocking in April—her face softened into a gleam of recognition, then a shy smile. When she spoke, the words escaped awkwardly from lips stiffened by a speech impediment. All at once we realized why she hadn't spoken to us before. Talking was hard for her.

Over dinner, we learned the story of a single mother with a disabled son who was receiving special care away from home. She missed him desperately, she explained.

"I love him . . . and he loves me, even though he doesn't express it very well," she murmured haltingly. "Lots of us have that problem, don't we? We don't say what we want to say, what we should be saying. And that's not good enough."

On Sundays she rode the bus all morning—same seat, same route, in and out—simply for the companionship of the driver whose name she didn't know, but who appreciated the hot drinks she unfailingly provided.

The bus ride was the best thing she did all week, she said. An occasional visit to the fish restaurant was a close second. "And this time I'm sharing it with f-f-f-friends," she added.

The candles flared on our tables, which were close enough to be one. Our fish had never tasted better. The night lengthened and grew cozy, and when we parted as friends—we shared names.

To have a good friend is one of the highest

delights of life; to be a good

friend is one of the noblest and most

difficult undertakings.

ANONYMOUS

STRANGE ENCOUNTER

BY

MAXINE ROCK

Dusk had descended quickly, and Sherry Apple knew she was in danger. Her hands felt numb on the steering wheel of her silver sports car, and fatigue was clouding her eyes. Doctors are trained to fight exhaustion, but Sherry, a thirty-four-year-old general-surgery intern, had pushed her body too far. She searched in vain for a rest area along a winding ribbon of highway between Atlanta, Georgia, and Louisville, Kentucky.

Sherry had been on call at Georgia Baptist Medical Center in Atlanta—with only a few hours' sleep—for more than two days. The pace had been unusually brisk: a youngster with head injuries in the emergency room; a four-hour surgical procedure on an elderly woman right after that; then rounds and more surgery. Now Sherry was zooming to an interview at the University of Louisville School of Medicine for a residency position in neurosurgery.

She tried singing aloud, but her throat was too dry. When she snapped on her CB to listen for the friendly banter of truckers, the airwaves were silent. She rolled down the car window, hoping that the brisk fall air would keep her awake.

Soon the hum of the tires on the blacktop became an eerie lullaby, and Sherry was blinking back drowsiness. Her car started to weave.

A lanky, forty-one-year-old trucker named Woody Key was fidgeting in the cab of his 18-wheeler. He peered at the empty road, wishing he'd spot a car with kids in the back seat. He liked to wave at the children, and if their car sported a CB antenna, he'd quack into the microphone, pretending to be Donald Duck. But tonight there was nothing to break the monotony.

Then his headlights picked up a silver sports car ahead. As he watched, it began drifting out of its lane.

Woody approached the car, honking his horn and yelling into his CB microphone, "Four-wheeler, are you all right?" His lights outlined a blonde in the driver's seat. Her head seemed to be bent forward, and panic began to boil in his stomach. *Can't she hear me?* he thought. "Wake up, lady!" he screamed. "Wake up!"

Sherry Apple snapped to attention, her heart pounding. She peered into the rear-view mirror but couldn't make out the face of the man who had probably just saved her life.

"Sorry to startle you," his voice boomed over the CB, "but I thought your car was weaving. I figured you were mighty tired."

Sherry swallowed, picking up the CB mike with a shaky hand. "I'm *exhausted,* and I'm lucky I'm still alive driving this tired. Thanks!"

"Call me Woodpecker, my CB handle," the trucker said. "I'm goin' to Kentucky. And you?"

"Kentucky."

"Well, good! I'll travel behind and help keep you awake. What's your handle?"

"Dr. Froot Loops," she told him. When he laughed out loud, she explained that was what the kids on the pediatric ward had called her. They got a kick out of silly names.

As the long miles unfolded, Froot Loops told Woodpecker that she was anxious about her upcoming interview. This trip to Kentucky was one of the final steps in a long journey that began when she was hospitalized as a child; she'd decided then to become a doctor. It had taken her ten years to scrape together the money for medical school. Now people at the end of this ride could shape her future—a scary thought.

"You'll do swell," Woodpecker told her. "Sounds like your patients really come first with you. Anybody would be lucky to have a doctor like you."

They swapped stories and jokes, and the time passed quickly. Woodpecker and Froot Loops parted near the Kentucky state line. She thanked him for keeping her awake and safe on the long, dark road. "Oh, that's okay," he said shyly. "I enjoyed the talk." Then the big truck rumbled past her, and the kind stranger was gone.

Sherry's interviews went well, but there wasn't much time to worry about the impression she had made on the Kentucky doctors. She was expected back at work immediately in Atlanta.

The grim business of surgical repair always picks up during cold weather when roads ice up. Though Sherry's schedule was even more demanding than usual, and she was often fatigued, she still insisted on being near her patients when they awoke, groggy and frightened.

On November 22, 1986, a Green Alert blared from the hospital loudspeaker: a trauma team was needed immediately. Sherry raced down the halls, her green surgical scrubs flapping wildly.

Sherry entered the trauma unit and found several other surgeons already bending over the bloody form of an accident victim brought in from a two-truck collision. Both arms and both legs were broken. His rib cage was crushed. His face had been smashed, and his left eye was exposed and hanging. Shards of glass protruded from his neck and shoulders. Worst of all, the man's skull was so badly cracked that Sherry could see his brain pulsing. She put both hands on his forehead, hoping to calm the thrashing victim.

The man was mumbling, "Happened so fast . . . couldn't stop . . ." He tried to move his arms and howled in pain. His blood pressure was plummeting. One of the doctors, working feverishly to stanch the flow of blood, said to Sherry through gritted teeth, "Keep him quiet! We could lose him any minute!"

Sherry began gently pleading with the man to bear the pain just a little longer. "It's not your time to die!" she whispered. "You're still young." As she talked, Sherry hoped her words were getting through.

The man did seem to be concentrating on the sound of her voice. Then, in a choked whisper, he asked her name.

"Doctor Sherry Apple," she replied.

"No . . . your CB handle."

"How did you guess I have a CB?"

"Your voice . . . I know your voice. . . ."

"My handle is Froot Loops."

"Oh, God . . . Don't let me die . . . It's me . . . Woodpecker!"

Sherry gasped. At that moment, more than anything in the world, she wanted to save the life of the man who had saved hers. *Is this why we met?* she wondered. She leaned over the battered figure and whispered, "It's not your time, Woodpecker!"

The surgical team was assembled, and Woody Key was rushed into the operating room. Sherry and a neurosurgeon worked on his head injuries while other surgeons repaired his broken body. Sweat rolled down Sherry's face. She and the neurosurgeon performed a craniotomy—a procedure to open the skull—to stop the bleeding and relieve pressure on

Woody's brain. Her fingers seemed to move on their own. Compress to stop the bleeding. Probe for skull fragments in the brain. Suction. Sponge.

The team labored nearly 24 hours. A dull ache throbbed in Sherry's shoulders, and her knees were rubbery. Could Woodpecker last this long? Could anyone? She had never seen such extensive injuries.

Each friend represents a world in us, a world possibly not born until they arrive.

ANAÏS NIN

The first days out of the operating room were excruciating for Woodpecker. He was bandaged from head to toe and still in critical condition. He couldn't move or speak. Then sepsis set in—a life-threatening infection that puts tremendous strain on the heart and other vital organs. He became delirious and writhed with fever.

Often Sherry would get home and find her phone ringing. Nurses, unable to calm Woodpecker and afraid that his thrashing would cause more injuries, asked Sherry to return. She always did. As she talked to him, although he was crazed with pain, he would gradually relax.

The weeks went by, and Sherry became convinced that Woodpecker would live, but she worried that he might be handicapped or badly disfigured. He underwent surgery to repair facial nerves. After that, Woodpecker faced many more operations on his arms and legs.

Then came agonizing plastic surgery to reshape his face. When the bandages finally came off, Woodpecker asked Sherry to take a look. She smiled broadly, and a wave of relief flooded over him. Despite some scars, his face looked fine.

Gradually the pain ebbed. Woodpecker learned to feed himself, his hands trembling as he clumsily grasped a spoon and brought it to his swollen lips. About two months after his accident, he left Georgia Baptist Medical Center.

On the big day, Woodpecker was taken down the hallway in a wheelchair. Then he saw Sherry, silhouetted by the partially opened hospital doors. He wanted desperately to walk up to her and say good-bye in style, but he couldn't.

Sherry forced a smile and whispered, "Well, just look at you." Her voice was filled with admiration, and she fought off tears.

"I made it," he said shyly. He reached for her hand, lurched forward and then fell back into the wheelchair. "It needs a little more work," he told her. "But I'll be okay."

Sherry looked at the man who had kept her safe on a lonely highway months ago. She touched his arm. This time, when he reached for her hand, his grasp was steady. "I don't think I could have made it without you," he told her.

Sherry's eyes filled. "And I wouldn't have made it without you," she said softly.

LONG JOURNEY HOME

BY

SUZANNE CHAZIN

"*A* letter arrived from your father," my friend Tomoko said, the thin airmail envelope crackling like rice paper in her hands. I nodded, but didn't move. "Perhaps you'll read it later," she offered.

I had arrived in Japan after finishing college. The trip was my father's graduation present, and he had talked excitedly about my returning home. But two months later I wrote that I might remain to teach English. I knew my letter would pain him, and I dreaded his response.

As I sat in the sparsely furnished room, I recalled tales of my father's youth, riding the rails during the Great Depression. He had been a hobo then, as full of wanderlust as I was now. If I had vagabond blood in my veins, I'd gotten it from him.

I thought about the gift that got my father to quit his wandering. It was my favorite story of his life on the road—and I could practically recite it by heart. In fact, I could almost hear his Brooklyn-edged voice telling it now:

He was twenty, traveling in a freight car across the western foothills of the Rocky Mountains. The other men in the car were scattered along the walls, their dusty faces as empty as their pockets. Their work clothes were worn, their hands callused from hard work. Each stared silently out the open doors as if he had some particular destination in mind. They were heading east, but they were all going nowhere.

My father had left New York a year and a half earlier. It had been easy to abandon the concrete stoops and corner stores of his neighborhood. There, young men worked odd jobs in factories, when they could find work at all. And old men—mostly Russian immigrants like my grandfather—whiled away their time talking about the motherland.

In Russia, my grandfather had been an engineer who spoke four languages. In America, he was a house painter. His friends were counts who now waited tables, and captains who now opened doors and hailed cabs. Late at night, they would talk of the armies they'd led and the banquets they'd attended decades before. They were men who walked in their own shadows.

Their threadbare stories filled my father with anger and embarrassment. How could they keep nursing one another's empty dreams? My father had bigger ambitions. He wanted to build bridges, rope cattle, sail the Pacific. California beckoned his city-boy imagination. There, certainly, people would see him as more than just a Russian house painter's son. He would return a success, he vowed, or he wouldn't return at all.

As the sun set and the train climbed into the Rockies, an icy chill stole into the car. My father wrapped his tattered peacoat around him and stared at his shoes.

They were made of rough brown leather and laced above the ankle. They had seen him through branding cattle in Northern California, cutting lumber in Oregon, hauling tuna out of San Pedro. They had hopped on many a boxcar from New York to California, and had paced the deck of a freighter as he sailed through the Panama Canal. Now the paper-thin soles flapped open—the leather as worn out as his dreams.

Another hobo approached him. "There's a man in a town up ahead who leaves his cellar door open for people like us." Dad nodded and followed the others as they jumped off the train. Plunging into the spring snow, he felt the icy crunch under his toes. Soon his wool socks were soaked and his toes numb.

A full moon lit the ground like white linen as the men trudged down the hillside to a small frame house. Inside the cellar my father found a corner to curl up in, but his feet were so cold he couldn't sleep. He tried massaging his toes; they refused to yield to his warm hands.

"What's the matter?" drawled a soft voice beside him. He turned to see a lanky man in his late twenties.

"My toes are frozen," Dad said gruffly, then pointed to his shoes. "These leak."

He was in no mood to talk to this stranger. Too many months on the road had chipped away his trust in people. Bosses promised to pay wages that never came. Men fought over spare change or a warm shirt, and sometimes stole them.

"Name's Earl," the stranger said. "I'm from Wichita, Kansas," he added, extending a long, bony hand.

"I'm Sol, from New York," my father mumbled, cautiously meeting his grip.

Earl began to tell my father about his life. His family had been wheat farmers for generations. But small-town living made him restless. Surely, he decided, there was more to life than working the land from sunup to sundown, marrying the girl you've known since grade school, and going to church suppers on weekends. Gradually, as Earl spoke, my father drifted into a deep sleep.

In the morning, they hopped the next train toward Kansas. By late that day, they were riding past the mountains and into the prairies. The weather turned even colder, and soon my father was stamping his feet to keep the blood going.

"Hurting bad, are they?" Earl asked gently.

"I'm okay," Dad replied tersely. This, too, he had learned: never show fear or discomfort—someone might take advantage of it.

"You got family?"

Dad nodded, surprised by the question. "A sister and a father and a couple of uncles," he answered. "Not much."

"Any family's family," Earl said, looking at my father closely. "You know," he continued, "I figured if I could just leave the farm behind I'd leave the farm boy behind. But that boy's still in here," he said, pointing to his heart. "I've had enough of the road. At least in Wichita I'm a farm boy with roots."

"Well, I don't come from a farm," said Dad, shrugging.

"Why don't you come home with me, Sol? My sister's a great cook." It had been a long time since anyone had called Dad by name. "Thanks," he replied. "But I can't go to my own home—much less to yours."

"Why not?" Earl asked.

My father looked down at his fraying jacket and worn-out shoes. How could the boy who swore to his father that he could do better come home after doing worse? "Because I left New York to be somebody, and I can't go back until I am," my father answered. He stared out the boxcar. It was evening now, and stars glittered like marcasite in a brocaded sky. Growing up by streetlight, he'd never seen such darkness. It made him feel alone. "One of these days, I'll go home," he muttered. "When I get together some money and shoes I can walk home in."

Moments later, he felt a heavy object hit the back of his heel. He turned to find one of Earl's thick-soled brown shoes lying on the floor beside him.

"Try it on," said Earl.

"Why?"

"You just said you'd go home if you had decent shoes. Well, mine aren't new, but they don't have holes in them either."

Earl dismissed his protest. "Just try them on, Sol. They'll keep your feet warm for now."

Dad slipped a cold foot into one shoe. It was a perfect fit. "I can't accept this," Dad said finally.

"Wear them for a little bit," Earl urged. "I'll let you know when I want them back." He tossed over the other shoe, then put on Dad's. My father laced them up and felt his toes tingle and grow warm as circulation returned. He had forgotten how good warm feet could feel. He drifted off to the rhythmic rumbles of the train.

Dad awoke at dawn. There were a couple of other hobos in the boxcar now, but no Earl. Panic-stricken, he asked the men if they'd seen him. "The tall guy?" said one. "He jumped the train at Wichita."

"But his shoes," my father said. "I have his shoes."

"He told me to say he's never been to New York, but he hopes his shoes get there."

Dad shook his head in disbelief. Among poor men, there is no greater sacrifice than to give up your shoes so another can walk. He had never seen anything like it before.

Or had he? My father thought about his old neighborhood. Mrs. Stoll, the landlady, took care of the sick, and Mrs. Roy, a neighbor, brought food to families when the breadwinner lost his job.

Certainly, they knew about hardship and loss. But they also knew about generosity—not giving what you have, but giving what someone else needs. It was an idea he had completely forgotten.

Give and take

makes good friends.

SCOTTISH PROVERB

Now, as my father stared at the Kansas wheat fields clicking by, he realized that Earl hadn't just given him a pair of shoes. He had given him back his faith in people.

That afternoon, Dad hopped a freight car bound for New York. When he arrived home, my grandfather, though not a demonstrative man, embraced his son warmly. And that evening, as he spoke of his days on the road, Dad caught the slightest glimmer of relief on the old man's face. My father sensed he had been waiting, fearful that his child would never return.

I opened the airmail envelope and pulled out a short letter. My father spoke of events, not feelings—he wrote about the sprinkler system he was building, my mother's new curtains, the dog's visit to the vet.

Then, near the end, he added: "My darling, stay in Japan as long as your heart desires. I want your happiness, and if that's where it lies, I understand. But you should also know that no matter how far you journey, no matter how rough the road, you can always come home."

Dad's words were a gift, as precious to me as Earl's shoes had been to him. They spoke the same language of sacrifice and generosity.

Things did not quite work out the way I had planned. The job I expected did not materialize, and my fascination with Japan waned.

So I returned home—not as a child obeying the blind tug of a parent's wishes, but as an adult, drawn by my own heart and the legacy of a gift from a hobo I will never know.

IN SEARCH OF SOPHIE

BY

EDIE CLARK

*W*e sped along the road to Tarnów, through clouds of car and factory exhaust, passing green fields where stout women and old men bent to the harvest. Andy, my driver, darted around wooden horse carts, happily practicing his English on me. "What is it you want to do in Tarnów?" he asked.

"I'm looking for a woman who once took care of my mother. Sophie Kordzinska." I pulled a worn airmail envelope out of my bag. On the back flap, in even, European-style lettering, was an address. "She's very old. I'm not even certain she's still alive."

When I told my mother I was planning a guided tour of Eastern Europe, her eyes lit up. "Oh, Edie, do you think you could find Sophie?" she asked. Seventy years had passed since they last saw each other. In that time, sea change after sea change had engulfed the world. Both had grown to womanhood, made homes, borne children and passed through dramatically different lifetimes. Still their friendship had endured, in a way I could only try to understand.

60

Poland is a big country, I told her, and I'd have little spare time. I felt it would be impossible, but said that I would try.

In 1916 Sophie came from Kraków to take care of my mother, Dottie, when she was a baby in Summit, New Jersey. Sophie was twenty-one years old, a slight, narrow-waisted girl with light brown hair tied in a bun. She was hard-working, a devout Roman Catholic who, my mother remembers, prayed on her knees in her room and attended church on her Sundays off. But what everyone remembered most about Sophie was her radiant smile.

My mother was often sick as a little girl, and Sophie fussed over her, sitting by the bed and cooling her fevers. When her young charge was well, Sophie took her for walks, and in the summer they rode the Ferris wheel at the Jersey shore.

Every afternoon Sophie tucked my mother in for a nap. But my mother would slip out of bed and tiptoe upstairs to Sophie's room. There she sat on the floor and listened to Sophie tell stories about Poland while working magic with needle and thread, stitching together petticoats and frilly underpants and silk scarves. These became Sophie's Christmas presents to the family. "On Christmas Eve," my mother would relate, "she had to make at least two trips to the living room, she had made so many gifts for us."

These are nice memories, but they most likely would have faded were it not for what happened. One day when my mother was seven, Sophie came into the living room holding a letter. She was sobbing. "My father is very sick," she was finally able to say. "He needs me to come home."

Within days, Sophie was booked on a steamer to return to Poland. "I rode on Sophie's lap in the back seat," Mother says. "We cried all the way to New York City. Sophie boarded the boat. The whistle blew. She stood on deck and waved. The ship got smaller and smaller as it moved away. And

she was gone." My mother still cannot tell this without tears coming to her eyes. "We thought she was coming back!"

For months they heard nothing. At last came a broken-hearted aerogramme from Sophie. Her father had met her at the train station, looking well. With him was a young man whom he introduced as Wladyslaw Kordzinski, the man she was to marry. He had seen Sophie's photograph and been so smitten that he told her father, "If you bring her home, I will marry her, and you will never want for anything."

But this was not to be. War came. Sophie's husband died of starvation. She was left with three children. A letter reached my family after the war. There was little to eat. Her life was one of uninterrupted misery.

My mother tried to help. Boxing up clothes for Sophie became a family ritual. Often the boxes didn't get through, but when they did, Sophie would write to us, overjoyed. Her letters were brief, and had sections crossed out by Communist censors.

Once, we received an Easter card. "The only happy years of my life," she wrote in her upright script, "were my years in America with your family. Here is very bad."

Now, a month had passed since I'd written Sophie to say I was coming to Poland. I told her what days I would be in Kraków and what hotel I was staying in. But I had no reply. Had she died?

Andy had never been to Tarnów. He stopped at a taxi stand, and several drivers crowded around, repeating the street name we sought. "Broniewskiego? Broniewskiego?" Maps were produced. A long conversation in Polish ensued.

Finally we started winding our way through narrow streets. We passed an open-air market where vendors sold enormous bunches of flowers. I asked Andy to stop and selected a big bouquet of yellow and red dahlias for Sophie.

Andy kept asking pedestrians, "Zofia Kordzinska?" No one knew of her. It was already after noon. In less than seven hours, my group was scheduled to leave Poland on a night train to Budapest. It seemed hopeless.

At last we stopped to ask an old man on a quiet street. He pointed. We were almost within sight of Sophie's house.

It was brick, covered with ivy, with a low fence around the small front yard. Sweetheart roses twined around the gate. "You must come too," I told Andy. "Without you, I'll understand nothing!" We approached, and I knocked. A short, plump white-haired woman opened the door, but she seemed too young to be Sophie. "I am looking for Sophie Kordzinska," I said.

Her face flushed with excitement. "Ees thees Eedie?" she asked, stepping out onto the brick path.

"Yes," I said, feeling sudden and intense relief.

"Oh!" she said, hugging me tight and dancing with me in a small circle. "Sophie is waiting for you!"

The woman turned out to be Sophie's daughter-in-law, Danuta. She led us through the yard (every inch of earth planted in vegetables, fruit trees or flowers) to another door. A tiny, aproned woman, impossibly old, stood inside. "Sophie?" I said. She put her hands to her face. Tears streamed. "Seventy years. Seventy years!" She grasped me and cried desperately into my shoulder.

They were prepared for my visit. Trays of cookies and plates of sandwiches were heaped on the counter. I introduced Andy and, through him, we began to speak. Sophie's son, Wladyslaw, joined us. The five of us sat around an oval table covered with an eyelet cloth.

Sophie's home was comfortable but spare. They had no car, no telephone, no running hot water and primitive toilets. But the house was nicely furnished. Chairs and tables were draped with embroidery. On one wall were two shelves bearing a few books. Proudly displayed in the center of the lower shelf, in front of a mirror, were two crystal vases.

Sophie sat next to me, telling me in broken English about her tragic life—about the war and how her husband had died, about how they were nearly sent to Siberia, about Hitler and Stalin. She let out a small cry of pain as she recounted how her sister, her sister's husband and their children had died in Auschwitz. She spoke of the son who had died just three years before from the effects of the meltdown at Chernobyl.

Yet, her faith had moved with her unharmed through these treacherous years. She had, she told me, prayed for my grandmother and mother every day without fail. "Each day, each day," she said. "Yes, even now."

It had not all been hardship. Wladyslaw had recently retired from a good job as an "engineer of buildings"; Danuta had retired after 30 years of teaching school. Sophie's beloved daughter Teresa, about whom she often wrote, was in Switzerland, where her own daughter was soon to be married.

I talked about my family and showed the photographs my mother had sent. At the mention of my grandparents' surname, Rahmann, Sophie began to cry again. "Mrs. Rahmann," she said haltingly, "Mrs. Rahmann was best woman in the world!" Her voice grew soft as if she were disappearing into a dream.

Her tears never stopped, all afternoon. We sat, talking as best we could, Sophie's wide, reddened eyes fixed on me in unending disbelief. We were strangers and yet old friends. I was an ambassador, a stand-in for my grandmother and mother. The love that came to me that day was unearned, but I tried to convey the place Sophie held in my mother's heart.

Leaving was hard. I gave her the flowers and small gifts I had brought from my mother—pink soaps shaped like scallop shells and some exotic shampoos. My mother had also sent some money in an envelope—"for my

Be slow in choosing a friend, slower in changing.

BENJAMIN FRANKLIN

64

dear Sophie." When at last I got up, Sophie hid her eyes with her hands and then, standing, closed her arms around me.

I was already out the door when she called "Wait!" and gestured me back. Slowly she took down one of the crystal vases—hourglass shaped, intricately carved, edges soft from wear. "For Dottie," she said.

"No," I said. She was giving me one of the few precious things she owned.

"Yes," Sophie said. "For Dottie."

When I returned home, I went to visit my mother. I showed her the pictures I had taken of Sophie and her family, and gave her the crystal vase. She took it in shaking hands and wept.

My mother is now almost as frail as Sophie. She is seventy-seven, Sophie ninety-eight. Their distant bond remained unbroken. I don't believe we have a word for this kind of love.

THE BOY WHO REMEMBERED

BY

JACK FINCHER

*T*ony Yurkew flushed. Why was his teacher looking at him, her lips pursed in dissatisfaction?

Tony, who was ten, worshiped Mrs. Hansen—tall, slender woman whose face normally wore a serene smile. He had felt this way ever since, in front of the whole class, she had tousled his hair and told him he knew the answer; he must simply think. Beet-red but grinning, Tony had thought hard—and solved the problem. From then on, pleasing her was the most important thing in his life. Now, what had happened? Where had he gone wrong?

After school, as he peddled magazines, Tony studied his reflection in the shop windows for a clue to Mrs. Hansen's disapproval. His ragged clothes and worn tennis shoes—hardly sufficient to shield him from the bitter cold—were not his fault. It was winter 1932, and the immigrant Poles and Ukrainians who lived in "Nordeast" Minneapolis had to make do with what they had, which was little.

Tony Yurkew's father, born in the Ukraine, had worked the graveyard shift at an iron foundry until the Depression struck and he was laid off.

66

While his father searched for work, Tony's mother wallpapered houses for a dollar a room. The family, then with four children, lived in an aging clapboard duplex. The rats that scrabbled in the dark, decaying walls terrified Tony.

Mrs. Hansen couldn't know about the rats, could she? Tony was mystified. He was a good student, and had done well for someone who spoke no English until he started school. That night, as he huddled under his covers, Tony decided he would ask his teacher what was wrong. She would *have* to tell him if he asked.

But the next morning, Tony's resolve melted like an icicle in sunshine. At noon, as he was putting on his coat to go home for lunch, Mrs. Hansen suddenly appeared beside him in the cloakroom. "Come with me, Tony," she ordered. Sick with dread, Tony followed, thinking they were going to the principal's office.

Mrs. Hansen walked briskly out to University Avenue and turned on Hennepin. She strode into the Minneapolis Goodwill store, with Tony right behind her. "Sit down," she told him. Tony sat.

"Have you got a pair of secondhand shoes to fit this boy?" she asked. The clerk had Tony take off his tattered sneakers and measured his feet. She was sorry that they did not. "A pair of long, black socks, then," Mrs. Hansen said, digging into her purse. Tony's heart sank. As nice as it would be to have thick, warm socks without holes, it would have been wonderful to have shoes.

Outside, their purchase in a sack, Tony started back toward school. Without a word, Mrs. Hansen turned in the other direction, again leaving him no choice but to follow. They entered a dry-goods store. This time the salesman had a pair of shoes that fit—shiny, new black brogans with high tops and real laces instead of buttons. Mrs. Hansen beamed and nodded. Tony gaped at the bills she used to pay for them— it was more money than he had ever seen. They took the shoe box and went to a café, where Mrs. Hansen bought a sandwich for herself and a bowl of soup for Tony.

As they sat at the counter, Tony tried to find words to express his thanks. But Mrs. Hansen's quick bites and hurried manner told him there was little time for talk. "We must go, Tony," she said. In her smile he again saw the serenity he treasured.

I will never forget this, Tony Yurkew said to himself as he watched her reflection in the mirror behind the counter. Back at school, he sprawled on the floor of the cloakroom and put on his new socks and shoes. *I will never forget you,* he promised.

Soon after, the school was closed; its pupils and teachers were scattered. Tony lost track of his beloved teacher before he had ever found the right moment to thank her.

In time, Tony Yurkew entered and finished high school, won a Purple Heart while serving with the infantry in Okinawa, and became an engineer, first with the Northern Pacific Railroad and then with the Burlington Northern. He married and fathered four boys. He also organized blood drives and for 26 years performed in schools and hospitals as a clown with the Fraternal Order of Eagles.

Then, in 1970, Tony suffered a massive heart attack. Lying in a hospital bed, he recalled his teacher of long ago. He wondered if she was still alive, and if so, where she lived. He thought of his promise, and knew he had some unfinished business to tend.

In August 1984 Tony Yurkew—sixty-two and the grandfather of three—wrote the Minneapolis Teachers' Retirement Fund. A few days later he got a phone call from Mrs. Hansen's daughter, who lived nearby. Her mother and father had retired 15 years ago and moved to Southern California. She gave Tony their telephone number.

"Hello?" He recognized the lilting voice of his former teacher.

"Mrs. Hansen, this is Tony." He found he had trouble speaking. "Tony Yurkew."

After he told her why he was calling, Ruth Harriet Hansen said, "Tony, I have a confession. I don't remember you. There were so many hungry, ill-clothed children. . . ."

"That's okay," he assured her, and it was. He told her he was flying to California to take her and her husband to dinner.

"Oh, Tony," Mrs. Hansen said. "That's so expensive!"

"I don't care," Tony said. "I want to do it."

She was silent a moment. "You visualize me the way I looked then. I'm old and wrinkled now."

"I'm not young either," he said.

"Are you absolutely certain you want to do this?"

"I've never been more sure of anything in my life."

On September 28 Tony Yurkew flew to San Diego. There he rented a car, bought a bouquet of long-stemmed roses and drove up the coast to the mobile-home park outside Escondido where the Hansens lived. Ruth Harriet Hansen, eighty-four, met him at the door in her best dress, her gray hair freshly curled, her eyes sparkling. Tony swept her up in his arms and kissed her. "Oh my, Tony," Mrs. Hansen exclaimed. "Roses are my favorite!"

Tony drove the Hansens to a country-club restaurant where they attempted to catch up on 50 years. Tony told about collecting blood and entertaining children in schools and hospitals. "I often thought about you and those shoes when I did those things," he said to Ruth. "See what you started?"

As they cruised back down the Pacific coast in the sunset, Ruth Hansen said, "How can I ever thank you for all the trouble you've taken?"

"Just think how much interest I owe you for the shoes." Tony squeezed her hand.

A few weeks later, Tony received a note in perfect Spencerian script from Ruth Harriet Hansen. "In my career I've had many commendations and letters of appreciation from former students," she wrote. "But what you did for me was the highlight of my life."

To a friend's house, the road is never long.

A LITTLE HELP FROM
A FRIEND

BY

DUDLEY A. HENRIQUE

The weather was beautiful on that November morning. The city of Fredericksburg, Virginia, passed beneath the left wing of the rebuilt P51 Mustang fighter as I rolled out on a heading of 330 degrees. Ahead was the place I was looking for, the town of Culpeper.

My altitude was 15,000 feet. Pushing the stick forward, I started the Mustang down in a hurry. I found the spot I was looking for, then rolled the fighter into a dive. The airspeed indicator showed over 400 m.p.h. when I eased out of the dive. I was at treetop level and headed up the correct country road. I counted three seconds and performed the finest climbing roll of my life.

I realized that I had violated a number of federal flying regulations, including unauthorized low buzzing, flying in illicit proximity to buildings and performing aerobatics under 1500 feet. And this by an official of the Combat Pilots Association and a play-it-by-the-book flying instructor! But I had no regrets about my single outburst of lawlessness. Right or wrong, that moment was forever mine.

I was six when my father divorced my mother and left us in New York City to fend for ourselves. It was 1943 and times were tough.

Mother was working in a defense plant when she married a man who became known to me as Jack. He was a man prone to fits of rage. Life with Jack was a series of loud arguments in the night, sometimes followed by the sounds of hitting. I remember my mother crying a lot.

One night Jack told me that he and my mother were going out and that I was to go to bed and stay there. Then he turned off my light and left.

I had a habit of sneaking out of bed and watching from the window as they drove away. As I was walking across the room in the dark, the light snapped on. Jack was standing at the door, holding a belt and a piece of clothesline. He cursed at me, shouting that I had disobeyed him. He threw me on the bed and tied my hands and feet to the frame. Then he beat me until I was bleeding. At some point the belt buckle hit my mouth, knocking out a front tooth. He then untied me and left. My mother must have heard what was going on, but I did not see her until the next morning.

I lived under these conditions for the next two years. Then one night my father's mother came up from Wilmington, Delaware. After a violent argument with my mother, Grandmother whisked me out to a waiting car and drove away. That was the last time I saw my mother.

For the next eight years I lived in Wilmington. My grandmother was a good woman but very strict; she almost never used the word "love" in conversation. Meanwhile, my father had remarried and was living in Texas with his second wife. He came to visit from time to time, but I hardly knew him. I remember him as a man who brought me presents.

Grandmother was a business manager for a large company and had little time for me. I would see her before I left for school, and not again until after 6:00 P.M. when she came home. At school I constantly got into fights with the other kids, and my attitude was surly and aggressive.

When I was fifteen, I was expelled. Grandmother enrolled me at a military academy in Bryn Mawr, Pennsylvania, which had a reputation for handling problem children. In a way, this was the first positive thing that had ever happened to me. The school force-fed me my first taste of education, along with fair and firm discipline. But I couldn't make it there, either, and I was expelled at age sixteen.

Back again at a Wilmington public school, I had weekends to myself and little to do. One Saturday I took a bus to the New Castle Air Base, which was located outside the city. There at the Delaware Air National Guard hangar I got my first close-up look at an airplane. It was a World War II P51 Mustang fighter. I was hypnotized! I walked around the P51 touching the wings and propeller; then I jumped up on the wing and slid into the cockpit. In an instant a man wearing three stripes on his green sleeve appeared and shouted, "Hey, kid, get out of there."

I was scared stiff and started to climb out. Then a hand touched my shoulder and pushed me back into the cockpit. Turning, I came face to face with an officer in a flight suit. He was standing on the wing; his hair was red, his eyes were smiling.

The pilot's name was James Shotwell, and he was a captain. Before I left the field that day he had become "Jim." Thereafter, I visited New Castle each weekend. Jim had been a fighter pilot in the Pacific during the war. After coming home he graduated from college with a degree in electrical engineering, and went to work for an engineering firm in Georgetown, Delaware.

The weeks came and went and I found myself drawn closer and closer to Jim Shotwell. I told him about the rotten time I had had so far. He responded with warmth and friendship. I had found my first real friend—and as a result my life was to be forever changed.

Jim and I would sit under the wing of his Mustang and talk about airplanes and subjects like math, history and physics. It was wonderful!

Perhaps most important, Jim introduced me to the other pilots. For the first time in my life I experienced the feeling of belonging to a group.

One day I told Jim I wanted to quit school and find a job. Suddenly he got quite serious. "Dud," he said, "you remind me of a blind sparrow. He knows how to fly but he can't, because he can't see. Even if he got off the ground he would bump into things that would stop him cold. He wanders through life accomplishing nothing. He has no sense of direction. You have *all* the tools, Dud. For God's sake, use them! No matter what you do in this life, you need to develop one thing: a sense of direction! Think about it."

Away from Jim and the air base though, my life was still unchanged. I continued to get into trouble and my grades were bad. Finally my grandmother decided I should go to California to live with my aunt. I told Jim about this. Several nights later, he came and talked with my grandmother for hours. But it changed nothing, and at the end of August 1953, I was on a plane bound for Los Angeles.

My aunt was very kind to me and tried to help in every way she could. I missed New Castle and Jim, but I did my best to adjust to my new surroundings. Letters from Jim brightened my days.

Then one night in March 1955, the telephone rang. My aunt answered. As she spoke I could tell that something was wrong. She replaced the receiver and gently told me that Jim Shotwell had been killed. He had lost an engine while returning to New Castle from a practice mission. He could have ejected but chose to stay with the plane, steering it away from the populated area—until it was too late to bail out.

Emotions I had never felt welled up inside me. I tried to hold back the tears but could not. Everything seemed fragmented and confused.

The most called-upon prerequisite of a friend is an accessible ear.

MAYA ANGELOU

75

Gradually I stopped crying and started to think of Jim and the many things he had said to me. His analogy of the blind sparrow kept coming back. I had always known that what Jim had told me about myself was true. But until that night I hadn't been able to piece together the puzzle my life had become. Finally, I fell asleep, waking at dawn in a cold sweat. My mind was strangely clear. Instinctively, I was aware that something had changed. Now I knew where I was going in my life and what I would have to do to get there.

That year I enlisted in the Air Force and became an air-traffic controller. The Air Force finished the job Jim had started. By the time I was discharged in 1959, my negative attitude had been reversed and my faith in God and man restored. I wanted to go places!

I hurled myself into an intense year of hard work and study, and obtained my FAA pilot ratings. Employment as a flight instructor soon followed. It turned out I had some talent in aerobatic flying, and through teaching and flying airshows every weekend, I developed a reputation of sorts.

By 1971, I had accumulated thousands of flying hours, flown more than a hundred airshows and lectured all over the country to flight instructors learning the trade. During those years I flew just about everything, including some experimental and military aircraft.

In the fall of that year, a New York doctor contracted me to ferry a P51 Mustang from Newark, New Jersey, to Manassas, Virginia. I carefully plotted a course that would take me somewhat south of Manassas. With 180 gallons of fuel in the wings, I calculated I could include an extra 30 minutes' flying time before arrival at my final destination.

On November 21 at 7:30 A.M., I climbed into the Mustang on the ramp at Newark and angled south across Cape May, New Jersey. There

I picked up a heading for Cambridge, Maryland. Reaching Cambridge on time, I swung to starboard and headed toward Culpeper.

The place where I violated the federal flying regulations that morning was the Mount Carmel Baptist Cemetery. There beneath a tombstone were the remains of my friend Captain James R. Shotwell, Jr. It had taken me 16 years to find the right opportunity to pay my respects to the man who changed my life. And I did it flying the same type of airplane I had been sitting in the day I met him at New Castle. That climbing roll was my cry of triumph and gratitude, the salute of the fighter pilot.

Today my wife still kids me about my flight over Jim Shotwell's grave. "The Day Baron von Leftover Led the Great Culpeper City Raid," she calls it. But she knows how much that moment means to me. It keeps alive in my mind two potent lessons: One man *can* make a difference in the lives of others—as Jim Shotwell proved. And you can accomplish almost anything with hard work, perseverance . . . and a little help from a friend.

The love of our private friends is the only preparatory exercise for the love of all men.

JOHN HENRY CARDINAL NEWMAN

NEIGHBORS

BY

JOHN SHERRILL

Jiro Ninomiya came to the United States from Japan at the turn of the century and bought a few acres of land just northeast of San Francisco. There, next to a palm tree, he built a house for his family. Behind this house he grew roses, which he trucked into San Francisco three mornings a week.

Across the road lived Frederick Aebi (pronounced A-bee), who had come from Switzerland. Like Jiro Ninomiya, Frederick grew roses on a strip of land behind his home. In time both families became modestly successful; their roses were known in the markets of San Francisco for their long vase-life.

Eventually their sons, Tamaki Ninomiya and Francis Aebi, took over the farms. Both families worked too hard to do much socializing, but each enjoyed the other's culture.

For almost four decades the Ninomiyas and the Aebis were neighbors. Then, on December 7, 1941, Japan attacked Pearl Harbor. And in California rumors spread that Japanese residents were to be sent to internment camps. Tamaki's wife, Hayane, was an American citizen.

Their children were Americans, too, but Tamaki had been born in Japan and had never been naturalized.

Francis Aebi, his wife Carrie and their two children walked across the road and knocked on the door of Tamaki's house. While nine-year-old Lina Aebi looked on, her father said, "We've lived across from each other for a long time."

"Three generations," Tamaki said, glancing at his own five children.

Francis Aebi made it clear that, if necessary, he would look after the Ninomiya nursery. It was simply something that each family had learned in church: *Love thy neighbor as thyself.* "You would do the same for us," Francis said.

On February 19, 1942, President Roosevelt signed an executive order that permitted the exclusion of any or all people from designated military areas. Speculation grew that it might be used to get Japanese people off the West Coast. Meanwhile, there were stories of stonings and boycotts of Japanese and those who befriended them.

When the news of the executive order was broadcast, Tamaki and Hayane immediately paid a visit to Francis Aebi to discuss the quirks of the watering system in the Ninomiyas' greenhouse. Francis assured his friends, "We'll keep the greenhouse safe until things are back to normal."

One afternoon in late February, a black car pulled up to the Ninomiyas' home. The Aebis watched as Tamaki was escorted to the car and driven off.

Later, the planned evacuation of all persons of Japanese ancestry, U.S. citizens included, was announced. In August the rest of the Ninomiyas were transported to a barren landscape in Granada, Colorado. The relocation center consisted of tarpaper-roofed barracks surrounded by barbed wire and armed guards.

Back in California, Francis Aebi had to uproot the roses and plant vegetables to qualify for a farmer's ration of fuel. In the Ninomiya greenhouses he planted cucumbers; in his own, tomatoes. In both, he left room for a few roses. "For tomorrow," he explained to his children.

81

The whole Aebi family labored beside Francis. The children worked in the greenhouses before school and on Saturdays. Even with their help, Francis's work stretched to 16 and 17 hours a day.

A full year went by. Then two. Then three. Occasionally a letter arrived from the internment camp. The best news was that Tamaki had been allowed to join his family again. His only son, David, cried when this stranger picked him up. Hayane knitted wool socks and sweaters for the Aebis. Another child was born to the Ninomiyas in the camp.

One day word came through the public-address system in the relocation-center cafeteria that the detainees were to be sent home. The war in Europe had ended. The Ninomiya family packed up and boarded a train. What would they find when they reached their rose farm, Tamaki wondered.

The train pulled into the station. There on the platform, waving his wide-brimmed hat in welcome, was a man so drawn and thin that his cheekbones protruded. Alice, the oldest Ninomiya daughter, whispered reverently to little David, now six, "That's Mr. Aebi, our *neighbor!*"

Francis and Tamaki shook hands a bit awkwardly, as if they wanted to hug, but couldn't quite. The Ninomiyas looked anxiously out of the car windows as they drove into the countryside.

Finally they turned into the crunchy drive and passed beneath the palm tree in the front yard. Tamaki and Hayane got out, followed by Jiro and the children. They stared.

There was their nursery, intact, scrubbed and shining in the sunlight—neat, prosperous and healthy. And so was the balance in the bank passbook that Francis handed to Tamaki.

Carrie Aebi came running across the road, followed by the Aebi children. Together the families stepped into the Ninomiyas' home, which was as clean and welcoming as the nursery.

There on the dining-room table was one perfect rosebud, just waiting to unfold—the gift of one neighbor to another.

Do not protect yourself by a fence, but rather by your friends.

CZECH PROVERB

A DANCE I'LL NEVER FORGET

BY

HILLARY HAUSER

A couple of years ago, I received an invitation to an important black-tie gala. I felt honored to be included, for among the guests were world-renowned orchestra conductors, important musicians and various patrons of the arts. I knew I'd have to find something appropriate to wear, but I had left this problem until the last minute.

Now I was in trouble. The day before the event, the stores where I live in Santa Barbara, California, were about to close. Hoping I could find what I needed in less than an hour, I was preparing to race out the door when my telephone rang.

"Yo, ho, ho, it's Uncle Weener calling!" came the familiar greeting. Jim Robinson, a sea urchin diver who was a great friend, always announced himself that way. And though I never knew exactly why, he called himself Uncle Weener.

I explained why I couldn't talk for very long. "Wait!" he said. "I've got something for you to wear. It's perfect. Guaranteed. I'll be right over."

Whenever Uncle Weener gave commands like that, a person listened. That's because he always considered his friends' problems to be his own, and he cared very much about coming up with real solutions.

Twenty minutes later he arrived—a tall, lanky man whose wild, curly blond hair looked as if it had never been touched by a comb. He was holding a brand-new tuxedo he had bought for a small fortune and worn only once. It was the most beautiful thing I'd ever seen—a black jacket in the softest of cashmeres, a pair of elegant silk trousers, a crisp white shirt, a bow tie and a belt with an exquisite silver buckle.

"Here!" he commanded. "Try it on."

I am a tall woman, but to be offered this suit of men's clothes was a pretty wild idea. It was also one of the most loving gestures I'd ever received from a friend. I don't know many people who willingly lend their expensive evening clothes to others.

Minutes later I had on Jim's tuxedo. He adjusted the bow tie, then asked me to put on earrings and a pair of high heels. Looking into a mirror, I thought I looked sensational—but still felt uncertain. "You don't think I look like a man?" I asked.

"No!" he insisted. He went to the CD player, put on a recording of Tom Waits singing "Invitation to the Blues" and then invited me to dance. We swayed around the living room until we heard the lyrics "And you feel just like Cagney, she looks like Rita Hayworth, at the counter of the Schwab's Drug Store." We fell apart laughing, which put the final stamp of approval on the scheme.

I went to the gala, and to this day people still talk about what I wore. Among my favorite photographs is one of me sitting next to a great orchestra conductor who was wearing the exact same thing as I. The photograph is a reminder of Uncle Weener's generosity and his insistence on how beautiful and sensational I would be at the ball.

I had met Uncle Weener by accident. My husband, a sea urchin and abalone diver, was coming back from a fishing trip in 1986, and in the dark he hit something in the channel—perhaps a log. The boat began to take on water through the gaping hole in the stern.

Jim Robinson was on the scene quickly and towed him to shore. The immediacy of his actions saved my husband's boat and maybe even his life.

From that day forward, Weener became one of our dearest friends. At least once a week he would charge into our house, take a seat at my piano and play his heart out. At sea, Jim's boat was the center of action—Hotel Ween, the divers called it. At night other boats would tie up to Hotel Ween, and their occupants would bring out the barbecues and share food.

Jim was a unifying force, the one who kept up everyone's spirits. An energetic man, he loved the ocean and diving more than anything. Whenever he was forced to stay out of the water because of illness or injury, he would become almost desperate: "The ocean is my life!" he would say. "I can't be anywhere but out there."

If I ever ran into rough waters, Weener would call me once or twice a day to see how I was doing. Actually he called all his close friends almost every day. "Yo, ho, ho," the message always began. "How are you? I care. I love you." He always said "I love you."

On December 9, 1994, Jim's roommate, Pam Schrack, came over to visit me. While we were having lunch, another friend called to say she had heard that a sea urchin diver had been bitten by a shark. Pam and I thought, *Oh, no,* but we were sure it was no one we knew.

Pam and I finished lunch and then she left. Minutes later she called. "It's Jimmy!" she cried. "He's gone!" Receiving this news was like falling into quicksand, where words sit on the surface, then slowly sink into some ugly quagmire.

I raced down to the harbor to be with Pam and Jim's other friends. We found out his boat, the *Florentia Marie*, had anchored off the west end of San Miguel Island. Jim had gone into the water with his dive scooter to survey the area. No one knows how deep he went, but when he came to the surface, he got a hand on the transom and said, "White shark! I got bit by a white shark."

Two fellow crew members, Ward Motyer and Steve Stickney, pulled him up and applied tourniquets anywhere they could. With their hands they tried to stop the bleeding from his mangled legs. Despite their efforts, he stopped breathing minutes later.

At three the next morning, my husband and I got out of bed, neither of us able to sleep. In the dark we went to the piano and quietly began to sing a Tom Waits ballad called "On the Nickel." When we got to the words "What becomes of all the little boys, who never comb their hair?" we broke down and cried.

No one in the Santa Barbara harbor will ever forget Jim's funeral or the line of people outside the church. As the minister read a passage from Ecclesiastes—". . . a time to be born, a time to die . . ."—a phone rang. Many people laughed, and I'm sure we were all thinking the same thing: it was as if Uncle Weener were calling once again, to say nothing more than, "Yo, ho, ho! How are you? I love you."

Then came the spreading of ashes from the *Florentia Marie*, with 56 boats following Jim's boat out to sea, and the flares and gun salutes that could be seen for miles.

Since then I have learned that my story of the tuxedo is not so unusual. It turns out that many people have a tale to tell about Uncle Weener's unlimited, no-strings-attached friendship. He went to bat for those who had no one else on their side. He was a father figure to divers getting started in the business. He loaned money even when he was low on funds himself. When he did have money, he insisted on giving it away, buying gifts for others and throwing parties for his friends. And he never asked for anything in return.

What is the way to immortality? It is not through naming buildings or amassing fortunes. It is through simple acts of kindness, of putting someone else's needs before your own. When buildings have crumbled and fortunes have been spent, love and selfless acts of caring live on.

The deeds of Jim Robinson continue to guide the friends who still think about him. *What would Uncle Weener do in this situation?* we ask ourselves. Maybe I shouldn't be so stingy, maybe I should take more time to tell someone I care, maybe I should organize some fun for everybody, maybe I should *live* a little more!

When I think of Uncle Weener, I think of a life lived deeply and filled with unconditional loving. But what I cherish the most is the memory of wearing his beautiful tuxedo and swaying around the living room. It's a dance I'll never forget.

My friends are my estate. Forgive me then

the avarice to hoard them!

EMILY DICKINSON

NO PLACE
So BEAUTIFUL

Special Feature

BY

KATIE McCABE

Rich peals of laughter echoed through the tiny Madison Valley Hospital in Montana, resounding from one end of the hushed corridor to the other. From inside an office marked "R. E. Losee, M.D." came the sound of two voices—one deep and gravelly, reciting a litany of relatives—

"I took care of your papa . . ."

—the other higher pitched and softer, answering:

"That's Jack."

"And his papa . . ."

"That's Jack S."

"And your Aunt Jacqueline . . ."

The list continued, and the voices blended, piling name upon name. On this snowy December morning just one week before Christmas, Ron Losee, the renowned bone doctor of Ennis, Montana, was huddled with his patient, counting with the utmost concentration not her bones and joints but the number of her relatives.

The patient, Jackie Ann Northway Kirtley, had had a lot of ortho-pedic problems. She also had a lot of relatives, and Ron Losee knew them all. He couldn't resist the temptation to take a tally of them.

Side by side the two of them sat, the delicate blond woman and the burly, white-bearded doctor in plaid shirt and red suspenders. They went back a long way together, the forty-three-year-old patient and the seventy-five-year-old doctor. He had known her since the night he delivered her, a preemie so tiny he could hold her in one hand.

Ron Losee had watched her grow up from a little girl who bravely overcame leg problems caused by cerebral palsy and learned to walk. When she married, he cried. When he learned of the birth of her daughter, Kelli Rae, he cried. And when Jackie's little Kelli Rae cried, he slipped jellybeans into her socks to comfort her.

"Doctor Lucy," Kelli Rae called him. But everybody else simply called him Doc.

"Okay now, let's see," Losee continued, "how many generations is it I've been taking care of your family? We got your little girl, Kelli, and we got you."

"Yup!"

"And then we got your mama, Kathryn. And her mama, Kelli's great-grandma. And then we got your great-aunt Zora. I took care of *her* mama, Ida."

"You did?"

His round face flushed with delight. "Yup. And that'd make her Kelli's great-great-great-aunt Ida. Five generations!" He let out a low whistle. "That makes your old friend here awful old!"

"No, it doesn't," Jackie Ann insisted, chuckling. "You just started awfully young."

Losee leaned back in his wooden chair and let out a big laugh. "Now we're horsin' around too much," he said, more to himself than to Jackie Ann. "We gotta get serious." Through all his passages as a doctor—from general practitioner to orthopedic surgeon to surgical consultant—he had relished nothing so much as these grand entanglements in the lives of his patients. And he worried about each and every one.

"So tell me, sweetie," he asked, his face furrowed with concern, "what's bothering you?"

"I know I need foot surgery, but I probably won't have it done," she began. "Because you don't operate anymore. And you're the only one I trust."

Outside Losee's office, phones rang and nurses rustled by, but he heard none of it. With an intensity that blocked out every sound around him, Losee listened to his patient. He leaned forward, adjusted his wire-rimmed spectacles and prepared to bear down first on the medical problem before him, and then on the real problem, her fear.

"You're the only one I trust," she repeated.

How often, over the years, had he heard that from the people he took care of?

And yet it had not always been so. There was a time before patients like Jackie Ann were born when Losee was an outsider to this valley, and everything he knew about practicing medicine was in the textbooks he'd hauled west with him from Yale. As for the business of "doctoring"—he had only a vague dream, a boy's dream, really, that being a doctor had something to do with curing people. And not much more than that.

He remembered it as vividly as yesterday. The year was 1949, and it was a late-November afternoon. As twilight deepened over the Montana Rockies, Ron and his wife, Olive, peered ahead in the blowing snow, trying to imagine the spot where their friend Buddy Little was driving them. It was a dot on the map called Ennis, and it was their last shot at a dream. The Pontiac coupe struggled against the fierce crosswinds that whipped through the mountains. As the old car sputtered up the steep, icy road leading to Madison Valley, the wind gusted harder, then harder still, whistling and shrieking. Inside the car Ron and Olive were quiet. There was so much on the line.

Until a few weeks before, it had all seemed so simple. They had decided to move west to start living the dream they had shared since Ron's medical-school days. Ron and Olive promised each other they would head to the part of the country they both loved, to do their doctoring and nursing in a little town, and raise a family there. They already had their three-year-old daughter, Becky, and another baby was due in the spring.

The West had tugged at Ron from the time he'd spent his college summers on his father's Nevada ranch. Olive, too, fell in love with that part of the country when he brought her out to visit. To them it was an untamed land, a world where everything seemed possible. Ron had ached to build a life there.

So for four months they had crisscrossed huge expanses of the West, only to find that the region was full of old-time doctors who either jealously guarded their turf or wanted to impose their own rigid, restrictive rules on anyone who offered to practice with them.

By the time they reached Oregon, their money almost depleted, Ron admitted aloud what they both already knew: they were out of prospects. "We gotta go back East," he said.

Exhausted and defeated, they'd pointed their car homeward, heading back through Montana. They stopped in Helena to visit Buddy Little, a college friend with a medical practice there. During dinner Buddy surprised them with an announcement: he had talked to friends in a town called Ennis, an hour southwest of Bozeman. They were searching for a doctor and were so eager for medical help that they had begun building a doctor's office with living quarters attached.

"Let's go take a look!" Ron said immediately. Buddy called ahead to arrange an interview, and they all piled into the Pontiac for the drive.

And that was how Ron found himself driving with his friend and his family down this strange road, tire chains clanking on the pavement.

Slowly the coupe chugged up the last stretch of an icy incline and rounded the curve at the top of the pass looming over the valley. In the seconds before they began their descent, the travelers leaned forward and looked down. Spread out before them in endless folds of white was a valley so vast and wild it made every other part of the West look tame.

In the entire expanse of blowing, billowing snow that lay between the Madison Range to the east and the Tobacco Root Mountains to the west, nothing moved. It was empty, untouched and, so far as they could tell from the mountaintop, absolutely unpeopled.

Before they knew it, the coupe flew down Norris Hill. In an instant, it seemed, they were swallowed up by the valley, at one with the vastness, speeding over mile after endless mile of snow-covered road toward—something. A "little cow town," Buddy had called it when he first described it to them.

At last, from out of the gathering dusk, the bare studding of what would become the doctor's quarters appeared. The road dipped, and there, plainer than plain, in all its roughness, lay the two whole blocks of Ennis, Montana, aglow with saloon lights.

Ron and Olive gazed silently at the raw little pioneer town and then up at the black-and-white mountain peaks towering over it all. Majestic and alluring, they dwarfed everything around them.

The darkness deepened as Buddy drove the family on, past the storefronts and bars and gas stations, and on toward the moonlit mountains. Through the blackness they followed Jack Creek to where it emerged from the Madison Range. There, in a sod-roofed cabin, warming themselves around a smoky fire, the people of Ennis waited.

The instant Ron, Olive and Becky stepped into the little log house, they felt the chill and darkness of the November night dissolve. The valley's medical committee had gathered there to greet them. "Come in, doctor. Sit by the fire! You and your family must be half-frozen," host Lois Bry said. Benches scraped as the people at the far end of the room stood and crowded forward, hands outstretched, to introduce themselves.

"Up to the table, everyone," Lois called. From great platters came sizzling slabs of elk meat—"just off the hoof," one of the ranch hands bragged.

When Olive asked for a phone book to raise Becky to table height, the crowd around the table chuckled. "The Sears, Roebuck catalogue might do better," said Lois Bry. Grinning, she held up the Ennis phone directory—all two pages of it.

Ron complimented the chef on the elk, and the men eagerly described the hunt for him. But he knew this was more than a casual dinner. It was the town's chance to get a look at him.

At first glance it was the most offhanded "interview" of his entire academic career. The group seemed to ask about everything but his medical background. Yet no admissions committee—not at Dartmouth, where he'd gone to college, not at Yale Medical School, not at McGill University, where he'd trained as a surgeon—had ever scrutinized him as thoroughly as the five men and three women who sat by Bill and Lois Bry's fireplace.

Ron was well aware from the moment he took a seat that eight pairs of eyes were marking his every word and gesture. When the committee talked about the tough life of cattle ranching or the advantages of sod roofs, they watched him hard. When he asked his questions about the winter and local road conditions, they studied him even harder.

They had reason to be wary. A whole string of slick M.D.s had come before him. They rolled into Ennis and stayed long enough to fish and hunt, but left before the blizzards came.

And so with each question the townspeople asked, they watched. And Ron watched them right back. In some intuitive way he felt drawn to these rugged, no-nonsense Westerners, so desperate for a town doctor that they were building free living quarters. It was a more than generous offer and yet, in a place that was 80 miles from a major hospital, Ron felt the town could put the building to better use. Without some kind of emergency medical facility, he and Olive couldn't properly do the job they wanted so much to do.

The fire had burned low when at last the moment came for deal making. Alice Orr, the town's gray-haired matriarch, turned toward Ron from her great wooden chair in the corner. The buzz of small talk quieted. Mother of the architect who'd drawn up the doctor's office blueprints, Alice was an ambassador's widow and one of the shrewdest, most respected ranchers in the valley. When she spoke, she spoke for everyone.

"If you choose to stay here," she offered, "we will build a place for you to live and an office at the edge of town." She took a drag on her cigarette, eyed Ron and slowly exhaled.

Ron looked directly into her sharp brown eyes. "No," he told her. "We don't want that. What we want is a hospital."

There was stunned silence. No one seemed to expect this answer. They knew the doctor was right. There at the table sat Claude Angle, who'd had to be flown to a hospital in Sheridan last winter for an emergency appendectomy. And there was power-plant manager Ralph Brownell, who had watched helplessly the previous March as a former employee died in agony from a blocked bowel because the valley was snowbound for three weeks.

For nearly a year, Ennis town meetings had raged with the question of whether a hospital or living quarters would be better "doctor bait." Even after the building was begun, the people were still deadlocked about what it should be. Now here was this handsome young New Yorker resolving the question for them.

"Are you serious?" someone finally asked, breaking the silence.

"Yes," Ron answered calmly.

"You *don't* want the house?"

"Oh, no," Ron said easily.

Under the smoky haze that hung low overhead, people shifted in their chairs as they revised their opinions of this newcomer. For all the other would-be cowboy doctors, the promise of free living quarters hadn't been enough. Now here was this Easterner, as sincere as anyone they'd ever seen, telling them they could have it all: a doctor and a hospital.

"My family and I will find a place to live," Ron continued. "We expected to do that. With all the effort you folks are putting into that building up the road, why not make it something we really need?"

The lines in Alice Orr's leathery face crinkled into a smile. She looked around the room and called out: "All in favor of building a hospital, say 'Aye'!"

The chorus of approval was loud, enthusiastic and instantaneous.

In a matter of minutes, the remaining details fell into place. Until the new doctor found a home, the Brys offered lodging in their house. Ron and Olive accepted. The skeleton of studding that was to have been the doctor's living quarters was re-designated on the spot as a tiny hospital. The blueprint's kitchen was now a delivery room, and the living room became space for five patient beds.

Each of the men and women on the committee came forward and sealed the bargain, Montana-style, with a solemn handshake, and Ron Losee was the doctor of Ennis.

Within days the phone wires all over southwestern Montana were buzzing with the news: there was a new physician in Madison Valley. From Pony, 30 miles north of Ennis, to West Yellowstone, 60 miles south, the word went out. Switchboard operators passed along almost daily updates: the doctor and his family were at the Bry ranch. He had begun making house calls. He fixed Grandma Evans's hernia and Nels Jacobsen's back, and was treating Lulu Grady's heart trouble.

With every move Ron made, the party lines crackled, until finally, the week before Christmas, the biggest bulletin of all went out: the doctor had found a permanent place in Ennis at Winifred Jeffers's log house on Main Street.

Within days, people were at the door.

"How on earth did they find us, Ron?" Olive wondered. "And so soon!"

"Damned if I know." He chuckled. "Where are we gonna put 'em all? Or examine 'em? All we've got is one Army cot."

His new patients didn't care that the cabin had no medical supplies, fancy instruments or lab equipment. They came anyway: mothers with fussing babies; ailing cowboys tracking in mud and manure; sheepherders and miners and rodeo riders with broken bones.

One morning in the midst of it all, Alice Orr and some of her ranch hands roared up in a pickup truck. Seconds later she was shouting and directing her men to bring in an old cowhide sofa, a chair and a homemade desk. She surveyed the bedlam inside the cabin and grinned at Olive as she ushered a sneezing boy to the Army-cot "examining table." Then she flew out the door, calling over her shoulder, "Just something to get you two started!"

It did help—but barely. The problem was that they had more to think about than just the two of them. There was Becky and there was Christmas only days away. Between their meager income and even more meager savings, they could buy a small supply of lab chemicals and have a few dollars to spare. That extra money was just enough for a blood-pressure cuff, or the wicker doll carriage Olive had spotted in a Butte toy store for Becky.

The blood-pressure cuff waited. But as Ron and Olive discovered, patients didn't. Not for Christmas, or New Year's, or good weather, or sometimes even for daylight.

Each morning in the predawn darkness, amid sounds of donkeys braying and cows mooing outside their window, Ron and Olive would awaken to the low murmuring of a crowd of patients on the other side of their bedroom wall. Out Ron would stagger, yawning and stretching, to be greeted by the sight of whole families sitting on the living-room floor.

"Take your time, Doc. Have your breakfast!" they'd call good-naturedly, then return to the business of exchanging gossip and cattle prices and symptoms. Olive passed around coffee, their neighbor Anora Goetz slipped in the back door with doughnuts, and Ron boomed out his morning greetings to usher the first patient of the day into his rear chambers.

It seemed as if every ailing person in the valley found his way to "Doc and Olive's." Against the background noise of hammering and sawing at what was now the hospital site at the top of the hill, he listened, examined, prescribed and advised on everything from boils to broken bones.

The one group of patients Ron never saw was the expectant mothers. They still raced over Norris Hill between blizzards to have their babies in city hospitals. Even though they trusted him to treat their older children, they did not trust him with delivering their next one. They believed their personal obstetricians miles away were still "the best in the Northwest."

January rolled into February, with no letup in the number of patients. Every day from 6:00 A.M. to 6:00 P.M. people filled their living room. "Sometimes I wonder whether they've been saving up their illnesses for years, just for us," Olive mused one day. More than anything in the world, she had wanted to be right in the thick of things, not a bystander to her doctor-husband's career. This was a little thicker than she'd imagined.

Sometimes she'd wince when she'd hear little Becky out in the waiting room greeting more patients: "Do you need to see my papa right away, like that lady over there?" Or: "What sickness do you have?"

Then she'd hear the door open and close again, and Becky's interrogation would be drowned out by the shouts of yet another family descending on the place. Occasionally someone would wander into Olive's kitchen to ask for milk for a baby.

"Ennis is a small town," she said to her husband. "Where are they all coming from?"

Ron shook his head. *What would they say at Yale about this houseful of bedlam?* he wondered. Cast plaster smeared the kitchen floor, the smell of ether wafted through the bedroom, and Olive sterilized surgical instruments in her pressure cooker.

Even when Ron was away from the office, ailing townspeople buttonholed him in the barbershop, the post office, the drugstore. They seemed to demand his undivided attention almost round the clock.

Many of his Yale classmates by now were ensconced in comfortable private practices. And here he was in the middle of the Wild West with patients camping out in his living room.

Yet he loved it—every bit of it: the country, the town, the make-do practice, the people. Most of all, the people. He couldn't think of a single reason he or any other sane physician would willingly immerse himself in this much madness—except for love. Without that, none of it made sense.

He wouldn't have put it in exactly those words on the long-ago day when he decided to become a doctor—but that was what it was all about. On a golden autumn afternoon in 1933, he'd stood on a grassy hill behind his grandparents' farmhouse in Upper Red Hook, New York, mulling over the challenge the town's new minister, Larry French, had repeatedly issued to the teenagers: what are you going to give to the world, to pay back what you owe for the privilege of living?

It was a big question for a thirteen-year-old, and it set Ron searching for an answer. From the time he was a little boy, he had traveled with Granddad Losee on house calls to villages up and down the Hudson River. He lost himself in biographies of men of science. *What better way to give back to the world,* he thought, *than saving people's lives like the heroes in "Microbe Hunters"?*

From that point on, everything he did was about becoming a doctor. After high school came the tough premed courses at Dartmouth, then the grueling regimen at Yale Medical School, compressed into three years because of World War II. Even his trips west visiting his father during college summers became part of his larger dream.

And then there was Olive, the pretty, dark-haired, brown-eyed woman who came into his life during his second year at Yale in 1942. Just beginning her second year of nursing school, she was smart and determined and, Ron discovered, as gritty as she was beautiful.

Ever since she was a girl, she told him, she'd wanted to be a nurse someplace where people really needed her desperately—maybe in Appalachia, but certainly somewhere in the mountains. Olive's "someplace in the mountains" became "somewhere west" for both of them once they visited his father's ranch as newlyweds.

There had been stopping points in Ron's pilgrimage between New Haven, Connecticut, and Ennis, Montana: two surgical internships at the Denver General Hospital, a stateside Army tour after the war and a senior internship at McGill for more surgery. But there was never much doubt where it would all lead.

True, his work at Ennis was a lot wilder than the more gentlemanly country doctoring he'd seen on house calls with Granddad Losee, and even further removed from the heady world of the microbe hunters. But for him it answered the question Larry French had posed years before: what are you going to give back?

Every minute of every day, the men, women and children who came to him for help reminded him that the practice of medicine was as much about heart as it was about science. They were scared, they'd tell him across the card table that was his makeshift desk. They felt awful, they said, listing their symptoms, and they didn't understand why. At no time at Yale was he ever taught the response he found himself giving, as he reached for one of his well-worn textbooks: "I don't understand either. Here, let's look it up together."

They would lean over the books with him and listen as hard as any med student, their questions taxing his memory, his training and his expertise, sometimes challenging his assumptions and his pride.

And when he least expected it, they humbled him with their gratitude. One day brought eighteen-month-old Mike Judd, who bawled at his penicillin shot, rubbed his sore behind as Ron cradled him, and told him through his tears, "Tank you." Another brought Kathy Gould and her fiancé Jack Northway, who sat blushing and laughing as Ron and Olive teased them about their marriage blood tests, then surprised the doctor and his wife with a wedding invitation.

Always there were moments he dreaded. Every day, people who should have been in the hospital in Bozeman arrived at his door instead. What to do, he and Olive agonized, with the dehydrated woman who collapsed on their bed? Ron drove a nail into the bedroom wall and hung a liter bottle of saline from it. Olive started an I.V. drip. Then they kept their fingers crossed.

For emergency suction equipment Ron rigged cider jugs with corks and plastic tubing, courtesy of Angle Hardware, and kept his fingers crossed even harder.

It was stopgap medicine, but so long as it worked, the people of southwest Montana did not care. They kept coming back and brought their children, their relatives and their neighbors. And Ron, feeling every inch the doctor one minute and no doctor at all the next, jury-rigged his way from crisis to crisis, never quite sure how he'd make it until tomorrow.

Tomorrow always brought another surprise, as it did one late-winter morning. The storm that blew into Ennis on the afternoon of March 10 had begun as an ordinary snowfall, but by midnight it had turned into the kind of blizzard that kept even the hardiest folk indoors. People bedded down their livestock, stoked their furnaces and bolted their shutters.

That's why nobody saw Gil Hansen and his pregnant wife, Jean, set out for Bozeman. No one knew that the frantic husband had tried to drive up icy Norris Hill so his wife could have her baby in a city hospital. No one saw him try to shovel his way through snowdrifts by himself before giving up and backing down the mile-long incline. And no one saw the Hansens return to a silent, dark Ennis, exhausted and terrified.

The voice that pierced the mid-morning bedlam belonged to Tana Rakeman, the druggist's wife. "Come quick, Doc," she called. "Jean Hansen is going to have her baby."

Olive phoned a neighbor to watch Becky as Ron ducked into his office, grabbed his copy of *William's Obstetrics* and began speed-reading through it, inhaling whole chapters. His entire obstetric preparation consisted of six weeks' instruction at Yale and six weeks of unsupervised experience as an intern. He had carefully kept the book for the day when he would have to deliver his first baby alone.

Obstetrics, with its responsibility for two lives, was his greatest fear. It didn't help that the text offered a litany of horrors: what to do if the mother hemorrhaged, if the baby breeched, if the cord was wrapped around the neck.

As Ron read, his insides quaked. They kept on quaking as he raced up Main Street to the Hansens' and descended the narrow stairwell to their basement home, and heard Jean Hansen screaming.

Suddenly there was no time for *his* fear. The woman who lay on the bed was frightened and in pain, and he was responsible for her life and her baby's. He truly believed that when there was a job to be done, no doctor had the luxury of fear.

"It's going to be fine, Jean," he heard himself saying, with such confidence he barely recognized the voice as his own.

When Olive arrived minutes later with bandages and obstetric supplies, she held one of Jean's clenched fists gently in her hand. "There's nothing to worry about now," she reassured the frightened mother. "The doctor and I are here."

Softly she kept talking to Jean as Ron took over, arranging a makeshift delivery room. Ron's voice joined Olive's, quiet, calm, encouraging. "You're doing fine, Jean," he kept repeating, talking her through the waves of pain. "Just beautifully . . ."

The doctor's wife, so pregnant herself she could barely bend over, never stopped moving as she helped her husband. Jean had no way of knowing that Olive Losee had been an obstetric nurse at Connecticut's Middlesex Memorial Hospital, but instinctively she sensed the cool assurance in her.

Now Ron's voice was authoritative and brisk, not betraying a hint of the tension he was feeling or his astonishment at what met his eye when he looked up at the basement window just above the head of the bed. There, squeezed into a tiny window well and peering, goggle-eyed, was a group of neighborhood children and their dogs.

Isn't anything in this damned town private? he thought. Then, out loud, to the mother, "Oh, wonderful, Jean. You're doing wonderfully. We're almost there. . . ."

At that moment, all thought of the audience overhead was wiped out by the sight of the baby entering the world—with the umbilical cord wrapped around her neck.

Ron had seen newborns who were purplish-blue from lack of oxygen, but this infant's face was almost black. Quickly he cut the cord and carefully unwound it from the neck—once, twice, three times. Within seconds, the baby turned pink and let out a mighty wail.

"Congratulations!" Olive called out to Gil. "You have a beautiful little girl!"

Ron, dripping sweat and beaming, lifted the tiny infant in the air. Jean Hansen looked at the exquisitely formed baby wriggling in Ron's big hands and breathed, "She's beautiful, just beautiful."

"We decided, if it was a girl, we'd name her Charlotte," Gil Hansen said.

"Charlotte it is," Ron grinned, queasy with the sudden rush of nerves and pent-up fear and just plain joy that he felt. *What would these parents think,* he wondered, *if they knew that this was the first baby I'd delivered in practice?*

Neither did they know the list of horrible possibilities that had raced though his mind in the eternal 30 seconds it took to unwrap the umbilical cord.

Thank God, he thought, for the precision of *William's Obstetrics,* for Olive's coolness and for the position of the basement window, with the Hansens none the wiser for the invasion of their privacy. And thank God for beautiful Charlotte, the newest citizen of Ennis, pink and full of oxygen and wailing for her supper.

If there had been a public-address system in Ennis, it could not have broadcast the news of Ron's first delivery any faster than the kids who raced home to tell their parents. By week's end, everyone within miles was aware of the new doctor's most recent triumph.

It was only one baby, but it was enough to thaw the frosty reserve of the one segment of the population who'd held Ron at arm's length: the expectant mothers. Now, along with the regular onslaught of colds, viruses and fractures, he was greeted every few weeks by a smiling new mother-to-be.

Gradually Ron settled into the hectic routine of his one-doctor practice. Like his grandfather, he made house calls, only his took him out into much wilder and sometimes hostile territory. He soon discovered that the gulches and canyons he and Olive and Becky loved to explore on Sunday afternoons during the summer turned into treacherous labyrinths in the sooty blackness of Montana winter nights.

"Leave a light burning," he'd ask his patients, "so I can find you." On many a cloudy, moonless night he'd peer along his headlight beams for tall grass peeking through the snow, trying to follow the road's edge as best he could. His eyes would search the darkness ahead for the telltale dot of lamplight that marked the home where a family waited.

He'd walk through the door and hear the relieved "Doc! Thank God you made it," throw off his coat and head for the bedroom—to treat a baby's fever, or hook up an oxygen tank for one of the old hard-rock miners, or wrestle a hernia back in place or, when all else failed, help bring a critically ill patient to the hospital.

There were other reasons he'd make his treks to the rough cabins and ranch houses. House calls that began as "quick checkups" on lonely old folks turned into evenings of storytelling over long meals. After one of his more terrifying obstetric vigils ended, the whole family gathered around and refused to let him go until he helped name the new arrival.

"You delivered him, Doc. You decide!" insisted Wilma and Vern McLean one night in July when Ron brought their son into the world. "Should we call him James or William?"

"How does Jimmy sound?" Ron suggested, feeling more like a god-father than a physician as the parents and the baby's grandmother nodded approval. The boy became James William.

There were times, too, when he was honored and touched by how much they trusted him. "We want you to do the surgery, Doc," Helen and Denny Wonder insisted after Ron diagnosed their daughter Doris's condition as acute appendicitis. "We'll drive her to the Sheridan hospital, and you can operate on her there." Denny Wonder turned to a friend standing at Doris's bedside and told him, "This man is the greatest surgeon in the Northwest."

They tugged at his heart, these people, and so did their valley, which was becoming *his* valley too. On his long night drives home, Ron would sit up straight at the wheel and stare at the sight of the sun peeking over a local promontory called "the Beehive," as it set the whole sky ablaze. To the east, towering above the highway leading into town, loomed the delicate accordion-folded peak of Fan Mountain, rising up from the mist each morning to welcome him back home. On clear nights the moon, tinted pink in the sunset, cast an old-rose glow over the tips of the Tobacco Root Mountains, just as it had his first night in Ennis. He had never seen a place so beautiful.

Always overshadowing his triumphs, however, was the specter of failure and death. Just three weeks after he delivered Charlotte Hansen, he lost his first patient. Erick Maybee was injured horribly when a horse fell on top of him, driving the pommel of the saddle into his abdomen and crushing his liver. By the time Ron reached him, the young man was already dying. Ron tried everything he knew to save him, and when that failed, he rushed him to the hospital in Bozeman for liver surgery—only to watch him die outside the operating room.

Sometimes all he could do was pray, as he did on the frigid March night he had to use a tractor to get through the mud to treat Ruth Skank. Feverish with a massive abdominal infection, Ruth drifted in and out of consciousness.

"Get her to Bozeman, quick!" he told her husband, Ermin. The roads were almost impassable, but they had no choice. Ruth made it to the hospital and survived—with only hours to spare.

Fear of not being able to do enough for people dogged Ron constantly. Each time the phone rang and he heard a frightened voice on the other end, the dread would rise in his chest.

He would rush out into the bitter cold, start his Jeep and roar into the blackness, his gut churning with terror that he might lose a patient. What if the morphine or penicillin he carried in his bag wasn't enough to fix the problem? What if he couldn't diagnose the ailment?

What kind of doctoring was this? Ron agonized. The frantic rush to beat blizzards, the transfusion emergencies, the gamble with people's lives—it was madness. Until he had a hospital, he felt he was practicing medicine with one hand tied behind his back.

The truth was that though Doris Wonder sailed through her appendectomy once they got her to the Sheridan hospital, she might well have died during the 30-mile trip. Before Jimmy's birth, Wilma McLean's blood pressure had been so high that she was at grave risk of convulsing during labor. She didn't, but she might have.

The town needed a hospital desperately. No one had worked harder than the people of Ennis for their five-bed hospital-to-be. Long before Ron's arrival, the medical committee had already been staging rodeos, auctions and talent shows to raise money.

Ron worked right along with them, once taking shamelessly to the stage as part of a talent-show fund-raiser. "I hate to make an ass of myself," he yelled to the crowd as he stomped out in his jeans and plaid shirt and cowboy boots. "But for the hospital, I'll do anything!" He played his concertina and belted out a medley of bawdy college drinking songs. They laughed, clapped and cheered, and—except for one or two of Ennis's senior matrons—roared hearty approval. But in spite of all their efforts, they were still short of funds. To make matters worse, long winter blizzards delayed hospital construction. There was nothing for Ron to do but wait.

Suddenly, in a way he could never have predicted, the waiting ended.

It began as one of those rare, relaxed evenings when the Losee household was humming with laughter and talk with out-of-town guests. From the West had come an aunt and uncle who'd grubstaked Ron and Olive on the last leg of their cross-country trek; from the East, Hugh Long, the dean of Yale Medical School, and his wife, Hilda. All of them were fussing over four-month-old Jonathan Losee as they basked in the brilliant August sunset.

Beer and medical stories flowed as Ron and his former dean and mentor relaxed. The talk grew louder—so loud, in fact, that nobody heard the distant growl of a motorcycle engine, or the shattering of glass, or the screams from the far end of Main Street. Nobody at the Losees' had any idea that outside Angle Hardware, Win Angle had accidentally thrown her brother Bud's new motorcycle into gear, sending herself through a plate-glass storefront and Bud into a concrete wall. Until Ron's phone rang.

One minute he was pouring drinks for his guests, and the next he was bending over two young people in a sea of blood. Gashes covered Win's face, chest and arms. Although some of her wounds were deep, Ron saw that as long as he could stop the bleeding, she wouldn't be in danger.

Bud Angle seemed in much worse condition. He lay on the ground, motionless, comatose.

A chorus of voices was telling Ron what he already knew. "It's time to open the hospital, Doc." They had managed to finish the shell of the building and much of the interior. In fact, Ron and Olive were hoping to open it in a month or two after they had bought some medical supplies and equipment.

"They got plumbing there."

"Yeah, Doc, the water's running."

"Come on, Doc."

Ron looked up at the crowd and yelled, "This is it! The hospital is now OPEN!"

With Win loaded in the back of Ron's Jeep and the comatose Bud in another vehicle, everyone headed up Main Street, past the Losees' house, to the hospital. "Better come up," Ron called to Olive, who stood watching. Handing baby Jonathan to Hilda Long, Olive was on her way.

A good fraction of Ennis's 400 citizens followed her up the little hill to the hospital. Some carried Bud to the single patient room, and others gently lay Win down on a cot in another room. Ron cleaned and sutured Win's cuts, then raced to help Bud.

In the tiny room where Bud Angle lay, his new bride, Janice, waited—white and mute in one corner. Claude Angle and his wife, Ella Mae, were in another. Papa Angle stood rigid and tight-lipped as Doc bent over his tall, handsome, athletic son.

There wasn't a sound as Ron gently lifted one eyelid, then another, shone his flashlight and watched for the pupils to contract. "It may be dangerous to move him," Ron had been warned when he'd phoned Deaconess Hospital in Great Falls to speak with Doctor Alex Johnson, Montana's only neurosurgeon. "Watch him, Ron," Doctor Johnson advised, "and wait." So, in the hushed little room, Ron sat with the family, and watched, and waited.

Outside in the hallway, pandemonium reigned. "How can we help?" the townspeople wanted to know.

"We need beds," Olive said.

"What about linens?"

"Anything!" Olive cried out. "Bring whatever you can. Sheets. Towels. Pillowcases. And pillows! We don't have a single pillow!"

Moments later, big, strapping Otis Crooker, proprietor of the Sportsman's Lodge across the road, came through the door. He was wheeling two rollaway beds. "Where to, Mrs. Doc?" he asked. She pointed him down the hallway.

Olive called to the women who stood in clusters around her, "We need food. And pots and pans. And something to cook on. A hot plate. Groceries. More sheets. Bring whatever you can spare!"

The word went out. Men unloaded tables and chairs from pickup trucks. Women jockeyed by one another with armloads of linens. Olive stood in the middle of the chaos, directing traffic.

In Bud's room the fading daylight at the curtainless window marked the passage of time. The Angle family restlessly shifted between Win's room and Bud's, waiting for news from Ron.

"Is it time to move him, Doc?"

For hours now, he'd been checking Bud's pupils. "Not yet," Ron answered. He paused, looking at shy, earnest Claude, and Janice, and Bud's married sister Roberta, who'd just arrived. "When it's time to take Bud to Great Falls, I'll go with you," he told them. "But I'm waiting until Doctor Johnson gives the go-ahead."

Throughout the night and all the next day, Ron kept his medical vigil. Hour by hour, Bud's condition worsened. His blood pressure had begun rising, signaling a dangerous increase of pressure inside his cranium. Unless that pressure was relieved by surgery, Ron knew Bud could suffer irreversible brain damage.

He realized there was no more delaying the long drive to Great Falls, 180 miles away. "This is it," Ron declared at ten o'clock that second night. He walked out into the dark hall and dialed the phone. "Alex? Ron Losee in Ennis. We're on our way."

It was nearly midnight when Ron and the Angle family pulled out onto the highway leading north.

While Ron helped Doctor Alex Johnson save Bud Angle's life at Deaconess Hospital, the people he'd doctored and counseled and sat with and sung with on so many dark nights were beginning to perform a miracle of their own.

It didn't look much like a miracle to Ron when he came rolling back into Ennis the next day, bleary-eyed and exhausted from the Great Falls drive.

Wave after wave of volunteers came to help Olive in the next few days. People came from all over the valley, their cars and pickups and trailers loaded with whatever they could spare. Some came to clean. Others came to help nurse patients or to launder soiled linens. Otis Crooker toted in trays of steaming food from the Sportsman's Lodge. Maurice Hickey hauled up another couple of beds donated by the newly opened Parkway Motel on Main Street.

The hospital was overrun with patients. There was old Clarence Althouse, with a gash in his head, checking in, just as Win Angle was leaving; and there was Darwin Pasley, who'd fallen into an irrigation ditch and broken his arm. And right along with the arrival of newly hired nurse Madeline Flowers came the event Ron had prayed would wait until they had a delivery room.

"She would never have made it to Bozeman, Doc," sputtered Pete Jackson as he raced in from the town of Norris with his very frightened, very pregnant wife, Johnnie.

"She's damn lucky she made it here!" said Ron as he timed Johnnie's pains and tried to figure out where he was going to find an extra bed in the next three minutes. Or two. Or one.

"The sawhorses," he yelled to Madeline Flowers. "Get a couple of the workmen's sawhorses. And one of the doors that hasn't been hung." Just minutes after the assembly of the makeshift obstetric table, the Madison Valley Hospital's first baby arrived. Ward Jackson, premature but pink and feisty, was just small enough, Ron calculated, to fit into a drawer in the linen cupboard.

It was a scene to set any big-city doctor's teeth on edge: a preemie in a linen drawer, "incubated" with a mechanic's droplight, lulled by the sound of drilling and hammering and sawing.

The hallway around Ron teemed with carpenters, plasterers, plumbers and people from all over the valley. There was John Krauss, the Jacksons' neighbor, who offered to drive all the way to Helena to borrow an incubator for Ward; Gen Hickey, who, when she wasn't sitting with her sick brother-in-law, took turns preemie-watching with Madeline Flowers; and Dar Pasley's wife, who helped Ron tend her husband and other patients.

Summer turned to fall, and more help kept coming—from local women who insisted they could scrub floors, cook and do laundry just as well for the hospital as they could at home, to men who stopped by after long working days in the fields to landscape the entrance before the ground froze.

Everyone in town was proud of the hospital and was ready to chip in. When Ron needed blood donors the night thirteen-year-old Steve Hubner was hit in the buttocks by a shotgun blast in a hunting accident, Olive knew where to go: the bars on Main Street.

She stood in the door of the Silver Dollar Saloon and shouted, "We need blood." Instantly the place emptied, and she was on to Oscar Clark's Bar, then Julie Erdie's. Long after Ron had the donors he needed, men were still coming in, rolling up their sleeves and standing in line, just in case.

In the weeks that followed there was no way to tell, amid the onslaught of babies and surgeries and heart attacks and accidents, just exactly when the little red-and-white frame building that looked like somebody's house truly became a hospital. But a case could probably be made that it was somewhere between the wild night of Bud and Win Angle's accident and the beginning of the bitter winter that ensued. That was when Olive and Madeline Flowers transformed the crowds of willing but untrained townspeople into an efficient cadre of volunteers. "The Pink Ladies," Olive called them.

They included big, gentle Nan Taylor, granddaughter of a physician who'd doctored in Virginia City in the gold-rush days; Janet McAtee, who came all the way from Cameron, 11 miles away; and tiny, unflappable Frances Womack, a veteran valley medical assistant.

They proved themselves one terrible night in 1951 when Wilma and Vern McLean's house burned to the ground. Madeline and the staff moved into action, calmly attending to three-year-old Verna McLean and her brother Jimmy and helping Ron treat the burns that covered Jimmy's legs and abdomen. Every day during the three weeks of the little boy's recovery, through all the painful changes of bandages, the team did the job with care and efficiency.

For all the nausea and sheer terror Ron experienced with every delivery, the nurses actually had him laughing on the blizzarding January nights when he delivered five babies in 48 hours. It was his worst nightmare: five mothers, all in the final stages of labor, all arriving at the hospital almost simultaneously, each one an obstetric challenge.

With a full team on duty, Ron was free to do the things only he could do. He could talk with the terrified mother-to-be who understood nothing about what was happening. He could console Bea Clark as she wept in pain and frustration during her long, difficult labor. He could tell jokes to calm Ginny Judd and Peg Todd.

When it came time for the quintuple delivery and he needed five extra pairs of hands, he had them. They didn't make it easy, his team of nurses and volunteers who never stopped coming. But they made it possible.

On nights like that, Ron could almost forget how alone he'd felt in the "old days." The awful experience of Bud and Win Angle's accident was a distant nightmare, eclipsed by the birth of Bud's first child. Steve Hubner, now a strapping fifteen-year-old, had become an Ennis legend. Town folklore had it that he regularly spat BBs across the kitchen, purging himself of the shotgun pellets from the wound in his backside.

"Yeah, sure, I spit a few," Steve assured skeptics.

Doris Wonder, minus the appendix Ron had removed in the Ruby Valley Hospital, occasionally pinch-hit for her mother as Becky and Jon Losee's baby-sitter. Although his legs bore scars from his burns, Jimmy McLean was unstoppable as he pedaled his bike through the streets. And every so often Charlotte Hansen, child of the blizzard, toddled across Ron and Olive's backyard with their two-year-old Jonathan.

Now Ron had a whole new crop of mothers to worry about— mothers who were his neighbors, his friends, part of his hospital crew, church members and his Sunday dinner guests. They weren't just "obstetric patients," and so he worried all the more.

Tiny, blond Kathy Northway wasn't one of the expectant mothers Ron worried about—at first. All he felt he had to do when he told her she was pregnant was to congratulate her, and remind her that he'd "known her when."

"When" wasn't all that long ago, really. Less than two years had passed since Kathy Gould and Jack Northway, who'd sat blushing in the log cabin while Olive did their blood tests, were married in a little white church in nearby Jeffers.

Ron remembered every detail. On that warm Easter Sunday he and Olive and Becky were still the new folks in town. Becky wore her brand-new Easter hat and swung her Easter basket, while Ron, camera in hand, stood in front of the church after the ceremony. On his signal everyone grinned his best grin, and he snapped the shutter.

Ron could still see Kathy, the tiniest of women, looking up at her tall, handsome groom, Jack, as they stood outside Holy Trinity Church. Next to them, in his best suit, was Jack S., father of the clan, with his wife, Nora.

There was no forgetting when Jack S. died, less than a year after his son's marriage. They had all known it was coming for months—Ron and the family and the oncologist who'd diagnosed Jack's cancer. As Jack grew sicker and sicker, Ron visited more and more often. Although there was nothing he could do medically, he wanted to be there for the big, kind man who'd been among the first to welcome him and his family to Ennis.

The night Jack S. died, Ron had kept the family company for hours, able to offer nothing but a little morphine to ease Jack's final suffering. When an emergency finally called him away to operate on a young boy with appendicitis, it was one of the hardest exits he ever had to make.

It had always been so with death. It was the one thing he could leave to no one else. "Gotta stand my watch on this," he'd tell Olive on those nights when he set out for some remote cabin in the mountains to sit with a dying patient until the very end.

But now, happy news. There was a baby coming to the Northway family. "My best guess is early July," Ron had told Kathy. Winter edged into spring. The May day when he and Madeline Flowers had driven back home from Helena with a truck full of fresh supplies for the hospital, Kathy was the last patient on his mind.

Then Jack Northway called, yelling into the phone that his wife's pains had started. She was two months early.

Ron prayed that the baby would come quickly, and she did. For that much he was thankful, because no infant as tiny as that little girl could have survived a prolonged delivery.

"What are you gonna call her?" he asked Jack and Kathy.

"We thought if it was a girl, we'd name her Jackie Ann," her father said.

"Another Jackie?" Ron exploded into laughter. "You've got so damn many Jacks and Jackies I don't know how you keep 'em all straight. What about calling her Kathy after her mama? She's the one who did all the work."

When Kathy Northway shook her head firmly, Ron knew this was the one family that wasn't going to take his advice about naming their child.

Jackie was one of the most beautiful babies Ron had ever seen. She was so small she barely tipped the scale at three pounds and looked lost in the incubator. Instead of wailing when she was hungry, she mewed.

The baby's stomach couldn't hold down more than a few tablespoons of formula. Ron knew that in spite of all the vigilance of the staff, Jackie was probably not going to pull through unless he found a way to put weight on her—fast.

"If only I knew more," he fretted to Olive. He gathered advice from his pediatric colleagues. And alone in his office at night, Ron read and reread the "preemie" chapters in his "Baby Bible," *Holt's Diseases of Infancy and Childhood,* until he was satisfied he knew the best and safest course.

Just beneath Jackie's skin, in the hollows under her tiny shoulder blades, Ron inserted feeding tubes to deliver a solution of nutrients that could be absorbed into the bloodstream. "I know those little water wings look awful funny," he told the baby's anxious mother about the bumps that were forming around the feeding tubes, "but until she can hold down formula, this'll keep her going. We just have to be patient." *Still*, he kept wondering, *is there anything else?*

He spent every spare moment sitting by her. There seemed to be no end to the waiting, the worrying: about the swelling around the feeding tubes and about the lingering effects of her extreme prematurity.

Somehow Jackie Ann began edging—ever so slowly—toward a normal birth weight. Gradually she became a baby who could take a bottle, a baby who, finally, could be lifted from the incubator and held. When June turned into July and she weighed in at seven pounds, Ron knew that it was time for her to go home.

The day she was to leave the hospital, Ron lifted Jackie Ann up and held her tight against his chest, just as he had the night she was born, put his big forehead up against her little one and breathed in the perfume of a well-scrubbed baby.

One tiny foot peeked out of the blankets, and he bent over to look at it. Everything about her had been miniature, but nothing smaller than the pin dot of a toenail on her baby toe. "Look at that!" he marveled. "It's a dot. A dot! I've never seen a toenail so little." Then he inhaled her perfume one more time and handed her to her mother.

"It's still a dot!" Ron boomed at Jackie Ann, peering at her toes. "It never did grow!" He chuckled, caught between two moments, one 43 years ago, the other right now.

During those intervening years Ron Losee the baby doctor had become Ron Losee the renowned bone doctor. One winter night in

1957 he knew the time had come to leave Ennis and go to the Royal Victoria Hospital in Montreal to study with Canada's master surgeons and pursue his great medical love, orthopedics.

There was another day, two years after he had left Montana, when he knew it was time to return. No one but Olive understood why he had to go back to Ennis

"Ron, go to a bigger place," urged his mentors at the Royal Victoria Hospital. But he didn't doubt for a second he had to go back to Madison Valley. He returned, eventually found someone to help in his practice and had time to ponder the orthopedic problems that fascinated him.

Back in the shadow of his mountains, he listened to patients who came to him in pain just as he always had—only now with a specialist's ear. He began to question the conventional orthopedic solutions to joint problems. More than anything else, the problem of the "trick," or unstable, knee niggled at him. For years he walked or ran behind his knee patients, trying to analyze why their knees gave way. It was frustrating because, like a car that refuses to misbehave in the shop, the knees always seemed to function perfectly when Ron examined them.

Then one unforgettable June morning in 1969 when he was manipulating a patient's knee, he felt it go out. Even before the patient yelled, "That's it!" Ron realized he was on the verge of solving a problem that had confounded the orthopedic world for years.

Again and again he was able to repeat the procedure that caused on-the-spot dislocation. He x-rayed the joint. Finally he solved the mystery of how the knee's injured front ligament let the joint slip, or unlock. He conceived a method for reconstructing from the knee's own tissue a supportive sling that stabilized the joint without stiffening it. The "Losee

Operation" they called it when Ron published his findings with two Yale colleagues in 1978.

Almost overnight, the little hospital began teeming with patients from the outside: athletes from Montana State in Bozeman, rodeo riders and ranchers. Finally, surgeons from all over the United States and even France found their way to Ennis.

For Ron, fame changed everything. And nothing. The people of Ennis continued to fill his office, bringing to him, along with their orthopedic problems, fears and questions about their health and their need to talk things out just as they always had. Just as Jackie Ann had this day.

"Oh, sweetie," he said, "it's only your toes this time? I thought it was something big. That's awful little." She grinned, and so did he.

He was remembering the many medical crises in Jackie's childhood, years of horrific surgery that corrected problems in her legs caused by cerebral palsy, but left her with a terror of any operation.

She was remembering how scared she felt about the foot operation Ron then had to perform on her—twice—after he returned to Ennis as a bone expert; and how, as she was wheeled into the operating room, he'd gently held her hand; and how, when she came to, he was there, standing over her, comforting her again.

Although Ron was explaining to Jackie Ann the procedure for the new surgery she needed, and that he'd be referring her to a protégé in Billings, they both knew the real reason she was there: for the soothing presence of the "Doc" of her childhood.

Even before she asked, Ron knew what Jackie Ann was going to say. "So you'll be there for the operation?"

Ron answered in his booming voice, "Absolutely." Then, quietly, he told Jackie he'd work out when he and Olive could both go down to Billings and be with her.

As he and Jackie sat talking and planning, outside his little hospital the morning mist rose and unveiled the snowcapped peaks of the Madison Range, stark against the winter sky. It was a quiet, windless December day in 1994, years since Ron had felt the pull of those mountains as he drove into Ennis for the first time, and since he had declared to a roomful of wary strangers, "We need a hospital."

None of them—neither he nor the committee—had imagined, as they shook hands in the firelight, how much more they would build together.

Now he and Jackie Ann sealed their pact, not with a handshake, but with a bear hug. Even so, the deal was pretty much the same one he had made over four decades before in a sod-roofed cabin: the people trusted him with their lives, and he gave them his.

Friendship is a strong and habitual

inclination in two persons to promote the

good and happiness of one another.

EUSTACE BUDGELL

"THANK YOU, MRS. CALABASH"

BY
CHRISTOPHER PHILLIPS

*T*he spring of 1982 was a bitterly cold one for citizens of Midland, Pennsylvania, and of neighboring communities in Ohio and West Virginia. In March Colt Industries, Inc., announced that its Crucible Stainless and Alloy Division, the only major industry in the region, was being offered for sale. If no buyer could be found, the Midland plant would be closed. By summer an operation that had employed 5000 workers at its peak was down to fewer than 1000. Prospects for finding other jobs in the area—35 miles northwest of Pittsburgh—were poor.

Leaders of the United Steelworkers Union Local 1212 decided to create a "food bank" for the neediest families. Several thousand dollars was raised through spaghetti dinners and church and business contributions. But organizers were still $2000 short of what they needed for the first food distribution.

At noon on August 5, food-bank director Jack Conway sat in the Local 1212 office of union representative Dick Fink, discussing ways to raise the money. Conway had other problems on his mind too. After

17 years at Crucible, the burly six-footer had been laid off in May. Somehow he had to pay for his two kids' college education.

Unbeknown to them, a woman who would dramatically alter their dismal outlook was standing outside the marble building. The diminutive lady appeared to be in her early seventies, although her smooth skin belied her age. She glanced uncertainly at the Local 1212 sign above the glass doors, and then walked into the lobby and asked, "Could you tell me where the union office is?"

Directed to the third floor, she walked down the hallway to the room where Conway and Fink were talking, and peered in.

"May I help you?" Fink asked.

"Here's something for the food bank," she said, and gave him a bulky white envelope that she'd been clutching in her gloved hands. "It's not much."

"Every little bit helps," Fink said. *Must be dollar bills she collected from neighbors,* he thought.

"Let me get you a receipt for a tax deduction," Fink told her.

"Oh, I'm not interested in a receipt," the woman replied. "I just wanted to help the laid-off workers in my own small way." With that she abruptly turned and left.

Fink opened the envelope and pulled out a thick roll of bills in a bank wrapper. He began counting, and as he did his eyes popped in amazement. The bills were twenties, and there were 100 of them.

"Jack," he gasped, "that nice old lady gave us two thousand dollars!"

It was by far the largest sum given by an individual. The men were afraid their unknown benefactor might have been so caught up in the spirit of giving that she donated her entire life savings. With only the bank wrapper and her description to go on, Fink did some checking. He found that she could afford the donation. She was by no means wealthy, but had saved a tidy sum and preferred to live modestly.

Unless she chose to come forward on her own, Fink decided to protect her anonymity. But a reporter convinced him that the public should be told something.

"Let's think up a nickname for her," Fink said. After pondering several possibilities, he remembered how comedian Jimmy Durante used to sign off his radio broadcasts with a tribute to an unknown woman. "Good night, Mrs. Calabash," Durante would say reverently, "*wherever* you are." But he never told anyone who Mrs. Calabash was.

The next day the Beaver County *Times* printed a story on the surprise donation. "Thanks, Mrs. Calabash, *wherever* you are," the headline blared.

No one dreamed the mystery lady would reappear. But on September 3, three days before Labor Day, she was at the union hall again. She went right up to the third-floor office. No one was there, so she sat down and waited. When local president Ron Friess appeared, he assumed she was the wife or mother of a laid-off worker inquiring about benefits. "Is there anything I can do for you?" he asked.

Mrs. Calabash stood and gave him a plain white envelope. She again declined a receipt, and only after she had disappeared did Friess learn that the envelope contained $2000.

On October 15 the gates at the Crucible steel mill closed for good, and 4500 steelworkers were out of work. The food bank was desperate for money.

On November 18 Jack Conway and a troop of volunteers were in the union-headquarters basement stacking 3400 Thanksgiving turkeys for families of union members. Around noon Mrs. Calabash, envelope in hand, entered the building, walked downstairs and tapped Conway on the shoulder.

"Excuse me," she said. "Could you help me for a moment?"

When Conway saw the woman in the black coat with the white envelope in her hand, his mouth fell open.

"I'd like to make a small donation," she said, handing him the envelope and turning to walk away. Conway gently took her arm.

"I just want to thank you for your kindness," he said. "You've boosted our morale more than you can imagine."

"My main concern is for the many young people who are having a hard time now that the steel mill is closed," Mrs. Calabash said, a little embarrassed. "God has been good to me. Now I have a chance to help." And she hurried out.

Conway opened the envelope. It had "Happy Thanksgiving" scribbled on it. As usual, there were 100 twenty-dollar bills inside.

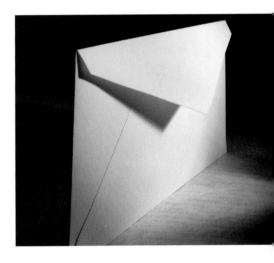

A pattern was developing. Mrs. Calabash always showed up before a national holiday, when the food bank, preparing to make a distribution, was in dire financial straits. She came before Christmas 1982 and six more times in 1983, once even making up her own holiday, writing "Happy Spring Time" on the envelope. Sometimes Mrs. Calabash walked in and gave the envelope to the first person she saw. This prompted Dick Fink to warn her to be more careful.

"But I trust everybody," she said. And her faith in people was justified, because her gifts always got to a food-bank official.

On May 5, 1983, a few days before Mother's Day, she appeared and happened upon Jimmy Lento, then the union's financial secretary. She gave him a white envelope, which contained $1000. "I'm sorry it isn't the usual," Mrs. Calabash said, shrugging her shoulders.

"God bless you," he whispered. "You're a beautiful woman."

Mrs. Calabash blushed. "Oh, goodness, my hair is a mess," she stammered. And she hurried away.

On Mother's Day, as a token of thanks, the food bank bought space in the Beaver County *Times*. "Happy Mother's Day, Mrs. Calabash," the ad read. "*Wherever* you are."

By that July Mrs. Calabash had donated $20,100 to the food bank, and in Beaver County her name was a household word. Midland's Fourth of July Committee wanted her to serve as grand marshal in the town's thirty-fifth annual Fourth of July parade.

Conway asked her, but she refused, shying away from publicity as she had all along.

"But I promise I'll be somewhere in the crowd," she said.

On Monday, July 4, practically all 4100 Midlanders lined the 13 blocks of the main thoroughfare. A red convertible led the parade. It was the car in which Mrs. Calabash was meant to ride as grand marshal. Instead, food-bank worker Anthony "Pidge" Pantoni was decked out to look just like Jimmy Durante, the Great Schnozzola himself—battered fedora, Punchinello nose and all. "Thank you, Mrs. Calabash" was painted in white on the sides of the convertible.

Pidge waved wildly at cheering friends and neighbors, but he suddenly quit clowning when he reached Tenth Street.

Maybe he saw Mrs. Calabash, maybe he didn't; he isn't saying. But his attitude changed to one of utter seriousness, and he called out affectionately, "Thank you, Mrs. Calabash. *Wherever* you are."

'Tis the human touch in the world

that counts—the touch of your hand and

mine—which means far more to the sinking

heart than shelter or bread or wine.

SPENCER M. FREE

WHO SAVED JOHN KLE?

BY

JOHN KLE

It happened so fast I didn't know what hit me. It was late in the afternoon of June 30, 1975; my friends Peter and Bart and I were sailing on Long Island Sound, plunging along in six-foot seas, surging before a 20-knot wind, the tail of Hurricane Amy. Suddenly a line tangled on the foredeck and, as I went forward to free it, a huge wave hit our stern, slamming our little boat to starboard. I went up in the air and when I came down, there was no deck beneath my feet and I fell straight into the water. I felt the shock of cold water on my flesh. I was not wearing a life jacket and, as the stern of the boat disappeared behind a huge comber downwind, I was filled with fear and the realization that, after 20 years of sailing, I was face to face with death.

I could see Bart and Peter struggling to bring the boat into the wind, but by the time she responded they were 80 yards away and I was just a speck in the angry waves. As I topped each wave, I could see them searching, and I waved my plaid shirt in the air, hoping that they would spot that tiny speck of color in the heavy seas. They beat up toward my left. I could see Bart on the bow searching for me as Peter struggled with the helm. Winds gusting to nearly gale force screamed in my ear, whitecaps slapped me in the face. I think: *They must see me now.* But they don't. The boat disappears from sight. I am alone. I think: *It is my time to die.*

Quickly, I discarded my sneakers and shirt. I remembered a trick from lifesaving class and made a float by tying knots in the legs of my jeans and filling them with air. Two 360-degree turns on the crest of waves revealed that I was near the middle of the Sound, about four miles from Long Island. It was now about 7:30 P.M. with two hours of daylight left. I must make a decision: Which shore? Maybe it is a homing instinct, but I strike out for Long Island, where my wife Debbie and I live. The thought of Debbie somehow eases the reality of my situation. Momentarily, fear leaves and confidence enters me as I set to the task: *Save yourself, because no one can find you in this storm.*

The pants float leaks its trapped air, but I manage to refill it twice before abandoning my jeans. Fatigue is setting in. Fear returns. Cold is the enemy. Already her icy fingers grip at my spine. Breaststroke, sidestroke and breaststroke again. At the top of each wave, a whitecap slaps me in the face and I battle the wind. I try to float on my back, but a whitecap washes over my face and I swallow a couple of gulps of water. Salt burns my lungs and my body contracts as I gasp for air. I am drowning; the water I've loved all my life is trying to kill me. *Stay calm, don't fight, work with the elements.*

My body responds, I'm okay. I think of Debbie, and just thinking of her brings new energy. I realize how much I don't want to leave her.

The sun is getting lower in the sky and the light is turning gold. I watch the changing sky while I do the endless sidestroke. This may be my last sunset; I am taken in by its beauty, blown clean by the high winds. The faint noise of a motor comes from somewhere. Turning, I see a small plane directly overhead. I wave, but the pilot doesn't see me.

I have been using the Empire State Building to gauge my progress, and there has been little. *Dear God, I've never asked You for anything before, but please help me now.* This small prayer seems my only hope.

As I keep working, new energy comes—from somewhere. There is perhaps 15 minutes of light left, and still so far to go. But I decide that if I die, it will only be after a fight, after I have given my all.

At dusk, I notice a small object in my path: a float for a lobster pot. It is a small miracle that I have swum straight to this tiny lifesaver. Ten yards to either side and I would have missed it. I grab onto it and take a desperately needed 30-second rest. The float is not spliced to the line, but tied. If only I can untie the knots that hold it captive! My numb fingers work at the knots, stiff with salt water. At last, reluctantly, the knots come apart. The float is mine as night engulfs me.

This tiny friend tucks under my arm like a football and barely floats my chest. Now, I can rest occasionally. I take a bearing from a bright light on Long Island shore—it looks to be about three miles away—and start out again with renewed strength and confidence. I swim endlessly, changing the buoy from side to side. I can rest only for a few seconds before my arms and legs become stiff with cold and fear makes me move on. I have never been so cold. Looking west at the lights of the Empire State Building, I can see that I am making progress, and from her bright lights I feel a new energy fill me. I estimate it is 10:00 P.M.

The blackness is suddenly pierced by the powerful beam of a Coast Guard searchlight. It shoots right over me; then a boat passes no more than 100 yards away. Looking around the horizon, I see the lights of a half-dozen Coast Guard and police boats and three helicopters as they search the waters for me with their powerful lights and dropped flares. I know that Peter and Bart are on one of the boats, and knowing that they are looking gives me additional strength.

Suddenly, the water around me explodes with light from a flare. I turn to wave at a helicopter hovering only 75 yards away and swallow the water spewing from a whitecap that hits me in the face. I lose the buoy in a coughing spasm. I cannot breathe. Then my hand retrieves the buoy and gathers it to my chest. *Stay calm. Don't panic.* Once more I can breathe. But leg cramps seize me, and I lose another full minute to the pain. I can feel my neck and lower spine starting to freeze. *Keep moving, or you will die.* Again, from somewhere, energy comes, and my tired legs start to kick. I start a rhythm: two strokes, breathe; two strokes, breathe. I'll hold this pace until the cold wins her battle and my fingers freeze and drop the tiny buoy. Then death. *Oh, God, I don't want to die.* Another surge of energy comes up from some strange, deep place, and it keeps me moving somehow—muscles on automatic. *Debbie, I need you.*

My leg hits ground. I don't have the strength to rejoice but only to keep my forward momentum up the rocky, low-tide beach. I get stiffly to my feet and, clutching the buoy, I stumble toward a nearby house with lights in the windows. I can't feel the ground beneath my feet; I have lost all sense of my body.

My numb hand turns a doorknob; the door is not locked. I go in, out of the killing wind, and call: "Sir, I'm in your living room!" The owner appears, and when he sees my ash-white form, he runs to get blankets. He moves me in front of the stove, feeds me soup. It is now 12:30 A.M. I get my story out through chattering teeth so he can call the police and tell the search boats that I have made it ashore. Soon Debbie arrives and takes me home: home to warmth, love, security, the future.

Shortly after the newspapers reported my story, I received a phone call from Buck, another of my sailing friends. He was very excited as he recounted the following incident:

"On the night you fell in the water, my wife and I were driving past the Empire State Building. We noticed a parking space right in front. Neither of us had ever been to the top of the Empire State, so we parked and went up. It was around ten o'clock. I pointed to the black void of Long Island Sound. 'That's where John and I went sailing last week,' I told Sue. Still talking of you, we put a dime in the binoculars and looked out into the dark sea where you were swimming right then."

As I listened to him, once more I felt myself taking my bearings from the lights of the Empire State Building. I remembered the warmth, strength and guidance those lights had given me. Had I perhaps been feeling the energy Buck and Sue were sending out to me?

A few days later, I received a letter from another close friend, Hitch, who was vacationing in the Caribbean. It was written June 30. He had been sitting on the beach just before writing me, and had suddenly been consumed by overpowering thoughts of me. There was no way he could have known that, more than 2000 miles away, I was fighting for my life. Again, I was transported back to that horrible blackness, to my desperate pleas for help, and to my hopeless feelings and fears, followed by the inexplicable confidence that kept coming back again and again to fight off my terror, and to keep me going. That energy was coming from somewhere: perhaps from that first genuine prayer I'd ever offered, or from those faraway Caribbean waters, or from the top of the Empire State Building, or from Peter and Bart, aboard a search boat—or from my small house in Sea Cliff, where Debbie was waiting.

Was I being tested that night—or protected?

Friends show their love in times of trouble, not in happiness.

EURIPIDES

I was still pondering that question when my friend Hitch came to visit us ten days later. He listened quietly to my tale, then went into the kitchen with Debbie to help her with preparations for dinner. A few minutes later he came dashing back into the living room, wild-eyed, with a frightened Debbie in tow.

"Look," he said, "you won't believe this, but the week before you fell in the water, I had a nightmare in which I kept seeing the numbers 9, 7 and 8, over and over. They woke me up, and each time I dozed off again they reappeared: 9, 7, 8. The experience frightened me so much that I told my sister about it. She urged me to forget about it, and I did, until just now."

He and Debbie kept staring at me. I asked what this was all about, whereupon Debbie went out to the kitchen and reappeared with the buoy that had saved my life. The small registration numbers carved into that buoy read 978.

A CANDLE FOR LORI

BY
PATRICIA SHERLOCK

*N*othing in the sweet and gentle haze of that mid-May evening held a hint of approaching sadness. An air of excitement hovered over our thirteen-year-old daughter, Ali, as she readied herself for the role of Margo Lane in her school's production of *The Shadow*. Ali's dad would be home from work in time for the performance. But just as important, Ali's best friend, Lori, would be there, even though her softball team was playing a late-afternoon game. "I wouldn't miss *that* for anything!" Lori had teased.

At first glance, Lori and Ali seemed an unlikely pair. Lori, a fine athlete, was solidly built, with dark, wavy hair framing a delicate face. Shy around strangers, Lori could erupt into a full-blown belly laugh when she and Ali got going. By contrast, Ali was not the least bit athletic, yet she danced gracefully, played the piano and loved acting. Far from shy, Ali had earned the fond nickname of Motormouth.

The two had met in kindergarten, but now went to different schools where they had both made new friends. Yet, unlike other childhood friendships, Lori's and Ali's bonds remained steadfast.

After the final curtain that evening, Ali's eyes searched the auditorium. "Where's Lori?" she asked.

But Lori had not come. She lay unconscious in the intensive-care unit of Valley Hospital in Ridgewood, several miles from our Oakland, New Jersey, homes. It wasn't until the next day that we learned what had happened. Lori had been overcome by severe head pain and nausea. In the time it took her mother, Trudy, to drive to the doctor's office, numbness and paralysis had begun to set in on her left side. An ambulance rushed Lori to the hospital, where the doctors diagnosed a hemorrhage in the brain. They were afraid that she would not last the night.

As I climbed the stairs to Ali's room, aware that I could not shield her against life's tragedies, I worried that it would be beyond her ability to accept what had happened. "I just spoke to Trudy," I began. "Oh, Ali, I'm so sorry. Lori's very sick."

"What's wrong?" Very sick did not register with Ali. Very sick had always been the flu or chicken pox.

Gently I told her about the hemorrhage and explained that Lori was unconscious and partially paralyzed. "You mean," Ali gasped, "like when Grandpa had his stroke last year?"

I nodded. Grandpa had died four days later. Now Ali understood. Sobs shook her body. I held her, silently cursing that I had had to shatter whatever vestige of childhood security she still possessed.

Lori slowly began to fight her way back. Within two weeks of the original episode, her paralysis disappeared and, to everyone's delight, she began complaining about "horrible" hospital food, sending her parents out for ice cream, cheeseburgers and bagels. Soon Ali was allowed to visit.

The two girls caught up on everything from Bruce Springsteen's latest album to their eighth-grade graduation dresses. Ali, beaming, announced, "The doctors say Lori can come home in a week or two."

137

She did come home. Each morning, Ali dropped a note in Lori's mailbox on the way to school. Coming home, she'd stop to chat. Soon Lori was able to come for supper. Things were returning to normal.

June came and with it Ali's fourteenth-birthday party. Lori was the first to arrive. After the girls went inside, Trudy got out of her car and came up the steps. One look at her face and I knew: *Dear God, this is not over. It is just beginning.*

Trudy told me that Lori had had a brain scan the day before. Where the doctors would have liked to see a clear picture—now that the hemorrhaged blood had been absorbed into her system—they had found a large mass at the center of her brain. Its character and location made it inoperable.

That warm evening, I looked at Lori in the midst of 14 young girls giggling and celebrating life. Her eyes danced and bubbled just like the others. Her smile was constant. *It's a mistake,* I told myself. *There's just no way the promise of her vitality can go unfulfilled.*

Later, when we were cleaning up, Ali said, "Thanks for the party, Mom. It was the best one yet. Last month I was afraid . . ."

The next day I told Ali. "Lots of people have brain tumors and live," I began. "There are benign tumors and even malignant ones that can be treated successfully." My words spoke the truth, yet the possibility of death was too real to ignore. While my heart was breaking for Lori, her parents, Trudy and Dennis, and her twelve-year-old brother, David, it also ached for my daughter.

"Will she die?" Ali asked.

"I won't lie to you. She could."

Ali stared out the window. "You know," I said tentatively, "Lori's going to be sick a long time, no matter what." I was torn between shame for what I was about to say and hope that perhaps I could lessen Ali's pain. "You don't have to stay quite so close to this. You can back off a little and people will understand."

"Mom!" Ali cried. "Lori's my best friend. I *know* she might die, but I don't really have a choice, do I?" In those simple words, Ali had said all that needed to be said. She did have a choice; she had made it. Ali was in this with Lori for better or worse. I dreaded where her choice might take her, yet I had never loved Ali more or been prouder of her than at that moment.

In the days that followed, I tried to convey to Ali my own beliefs about what was happening—that it was not "God's will," for I cannot trust in a God who wills human suffering. I believe that what happens to us happens because we live on this imperfect planet, in these imperfect bodies. What faith gives us is not solutions, but strength to endure and confidence that death does not end life, but merely changes it. I wanted Ali to come through with her sense of joy intact—still able to find life worthwhile.

Lori and her parents began a round of consultations with eminent neurologists in New York City. All agreed that the tumor was inoperable, and they put Lori on medication to control inflammation and possible seizures.

That June, while we sensed that life was changing in some irrevocable way, in another way it remained familiar. Both girls graduated from eighth grade, and summer saw them together almost daily. They swam in Lori's pool, listened to their records, tried on new clothes. They never seemed to stop talking, laughing and eating; only in passing did they mention Lori's condition. It was merely an annoying inconvenience that was temporarily keeping her from playing softball.

At the end of July, Lori developed dizziness and headaches. She was admitted to a New York hospital where tests showed the tumor was growing. The doctors repeated the diagnosis: the tumor could not be removed by surgery.

Friendships multiply joys and divide griefs.

A. H. BOHN

139

Lori was then sent to yet another neurosurgeon who believed he could perform a biopsy and remove enough of the tumor so that radiation could be started.

So, on August 3, Lori went into surgery at New York Hospital-Cornell Medical Center in New York. That night Trudy called. Lori had come through. Part of the tumor had been removed and a shunt implanted to relieve pressure. Once the biopsy report was in and the stitches healed, Lori could begin radiation.

Ali was quiet until I told her that when Lori had awakened in the recovery room, the first thing she asked for was a bagel. Ali laughed. "Now I know she's okay!"

The next day Lori and Ali were able to talk briefly on the phone. Our hopes soared. Lori seemed so well. If only the tumor proved to be benign, if only it would respond to radiation, if only . . .

But it was not to be. The biopsy confirmed an earlier suspicion that Lori's tumor was malignant. Radiation would be a palliative measure.

Lori remained in the hospital. When her stitches healed, radiation was begun. Although it made her sick to her stomach, she tried not to complain. Even in the midst of her nausea, she craved a Big Mac "with the works."

Ali had continued her participation in a teenage summer-theater group and outwardly her life seemed free of turmoil. It was only on Sundays after mass that her heartache showed. "I'll be right back," she would say. "I'm going to light a candle for Lori."

On August 14, Lori came home, wobbly but still bouncy. A sailor hat covered her partially shaved head. When she pulled it off to show us her stitches, she and Ali were already trying to invent a new hairdo for Lori's remaining hair. They never got the chance.

On August 15, Lori awoke with a splitting headache and was rushed back to the New York hospital. Emergency surgery was performed, and her shunt readjusted to relieve the increasing pressure. A few days later Lori stopped breathing and was placed on a respirator until her own system took over—the tumor was pressing on the nerve center in her brain that controlled respiration. When the immediate crisis had passed, Trudy found the courage to challenge the doctors.

"Have you ever known a person to survive with this kind of tumor?" she asked. Sadly, they answered no. "Then she's in God's hands. If Lori stops breathing again, we don't want a respirator."

In the early-morning hours of August 28, 1981, Lori woke up and told her dad she wanted some ice cream. "What kind?" he asked.

"Vanilla," she answered.

Dennis brought the ice cream. Lori ate it, went back to sleep and died peacefully in her father's arms.

The devastation I felt could only begin to approach that of Trudy, Dennis and David. And what must Ali be feeling over the death of her best friend? I had learned that a parent can't shield a child from all pain, but in the days that followed I also learned I didn't have to. Ali had a strength that sustained her, but I didn't know quite what it was.

About two days after the funeral, Ali handed me a letter she'd written to Lori's family. As I read it, I began to understand my daughter.

Dear Trudy, Dennis and Davey,

The three of you were all a part of what will probably be the happiest time in my life and I want to see you, not just as much as before, but more than before. I've had many friends, but none of them stuck with me like Lori did. She was the best friend anyone could hope for. She always wanted me to have what I wanted for myself. Whatever it was, Lori was there rooting for me!

Right now as I'm writing this, Lori may not be in the chair next to me, but she's with me in my head and in my heart. Something Lori and I did a lot of was laugh, so now when I remember her, it's mostly the laughter we shared that I remember.

Lori and I never tired of each other's company. We had something special. I don't know exactly what it was, but it seemed sort of magical! I know that that magic will be between the two of us forever.

I'm losing a lot by losing Lori, but just think how much I've gained from knowing her as well as I did. Thanks for being so wonderful and for helping me through this tough time. I love you all.

Love, Ali

I hadn't known that a fourteen-year-old could grasp the meaning of life so clearly. Beyond her grief Ali would remember that she and Lori had shared something special and been wise enough to recognize it. They had a friendship they both knew was a gift—a magic moment of love that would last forever.

Could we see when and where we are to

meet again, we would be more tender when

we bid our friends good-bye.

MARIE LOUISE LA RAMEE

SEND SOMEONE
A SMILE

BY

ANN BATEMAN

One day shortly after my third child was born, I received a note from another young mother, a friend of mine who lived just three blocks from me. We hadn't seen each other all winter.

"Hi, friend," she wrote. "I think of you often. Someday we'll have time to spend together like in the old days. Keep plugging. I know you're a super mother. See you soon, I hope." It was signed: "Your friend on hold, Sue Ann."

The few words lifted my spirits and added a soothing ointment of love to a hectic day. I remember thinking, *Thanks, Sue Ann. I needed that.*

The next day was my errand day, because my husband was home to tend the children. I decided to visit a card shop a few miles away that was having a sale. I wasn't in a good mood. The baby had a cold, and I was in a hurry.

Instead of reacting to my brusqueness, the saleswoman was extremely courteous and helpful. Noticing that her name tag read Janet Sullivan, I asked the woman if she was the store owner. "Oh, no," she said. "I'm just one of the employees, but I love it here." I left the shop feeling more able to cope.

On the way home, I thought, *I really ought to write a note to the owner of that shop and tell her what a good employee Janet Sullivan is. But, of course, there isn't time.*

When I arrived home, however, things seemed peaceful. On my desk I saw my friend Sue Ann's note. If she had the time to lift my spirits, why, I had time to help cheer others.

"Dear Store Owner," I wrote. "It was a hectic morning and I came into your shop with a chip on my shoulder. But Janet Sullivan was pleasant, extremely helpful, and she did not let my uptight mood affect her kindness to me. Thank you for hiring such a lovely lady and for making my day better." I signed the note "A satisfied customer."

Next I wrote to Janet Sullivan. It all took only a few minutes, but the rest of my day seemed to glide by more smoothly than usual. I decided I would write notes more often when I ran into people who were doing a good job.

That Monday my six-year-old came home from school with a clever puppet and several other delightful learning tools. For quite a while, I had been impressed with the good job Meagan's teacher was doing, yet I had never told her.

Why not? I thought, as I pulled out another sheet of stationery.

"Dear Miss Patrick," I began. "Your clever ideas make learning fun. My daughter loves school. You seem to have time for the individual child, and I frankly don't know how you do it. I'm so happy that there are dedicated teachers like you who have talent and love for their jobs. Thanks for giving my little girl a good start and a good attitude toward learning.

Sincerely, A Happy Mom."

I decided not to sign the note. I didn't want Miss Patrick to think I was trying to help my daughter to be better-liked.

When I went out to mail Miss Patrick's note, I noticed a neighbor checking his mailbox. Mr. Williams's head drooped and his pace seemed slower as he shuffled back to his house empty-handed. I hurried back into my own house because I could hear my baby crying, but I couldn't get Mr. Williams off my mind. It wasn't a check he was waiting for; he was quite well-to-do. He was probably looking for some love in his mailbox.

While Meagan drew a picture of a mailbox with a smile in it and Tami drew a rainbow, I wrote a little note. "We are your secret admirers," it began. We added a favorite story and a poem. "Expect to hear from us often," I wrote on the envelope.

The next day my children and I watched Mr. Williams take out his mail and open the envelope right in the driveway. Even at a distance, we could see he was smiling.

My mind began reeling when I thought of all the people who could use smiles in their mailboxes. What about the fifteen-year-old Down's-syndrome girl near my parents whose birthday was coming up? The people in the rest home near our house? The invalid woman in our old neighborhood? The endless people I didn't even know who still believe in courtesy and in doing a good job? Even on busy days I could find the time to write at least one note.

Hundreds of notes later, I have made two discoveries:

I. Notes don't need to be long. When my neighbors the Linthrops moved, I heard several other neighbors comment on how much they missed them. My note from our street was extremely short.

"Dear Linthrops," I wrote. "When you moved, you took some sunshine with you. People here miss your smiles and happy voices. Please come back to visit your friend on Cherry Lane."

2. Anonymous notes leave others free of obligation. It is difficult for people to accept compliments or help, and anonymous notes alleviate any embarrassment or feelings that they must acknowledge or reciprocate in any way.

At first I wanted credit for the notes. But, now, writing them in secret adds a sense of adventure. It's more fun. I once overheard talk of the Phantom Note Lady. They were discussing me, but they didn't know, and I wasn't telling.

Perhaps I will never have the means and the time to help others in magnificent ways, even after our children are grown. But right now it is satisfying to know that I am helping to lift spirits in small ways. I have found that it is easy to find the time to write letters of praise, love and appreciation. And as a side effect, I find myself looking at my own circumstances in a much more positive light. But then happiness usually is a side effect.

Age appears best in four things: old wood to burn, old wine to drink, old friends to trust and old authors to read.

FRANCIS BACON

JAMEL'S WAY OUT

BY

COLLIN PERRY

Three-year-old Jamel Oeser-Sweat sat huddled with his mother, Jeanne, on the tattered sofa. The building's boiler was down again, and outside their icy apartment an angry winter wind swept through New York's South Bronx slums.

As she rocked Jamel, Jeanne read aloud from a dog-eared copy of *Dumbo*, and the boy felt himself transported on the elephant's ears to far-off places. His mother treated him to a book nearly every night, and Jamel had learned to identify written words by age two.

Fairy tales were Jamel's favorite—particularly ragged, abused Cinderella whisked off to a ball in magic slippers. Or sometimes, staring into a mirror at his soft, nut-brown features—half black from his father's side, half American Indian from his mother's—he would imagine falling through the looking glass into Alice's world.

Now, from an adjacent bedroom, Jamel heard a loud moan. His father was in the late stages of cancer. Jamel picked up his book and tottered into the bedroom after his mother. Tugging on her dress, he asked if his father would like to hear him read.

"Hush, child. Your daddy's too sick for books."

"No," his father whispered. "Let the boy read." With a supreme effort, Jamel's father reached out and held him tight. "You keep using that head of yours," he said with tears in his eyes. "Keep reading them books. You got that, son?"

A few weeks later, an ambulance drove up to the building, and men dressed in white carried his father away. Jamel never saw him again.

In the years to come, Jamel would experience more than most people see in a lifetime. He would watch his mother struggle with mental illness; he would join the drug trade, witness murders, observe children become addicted to crack. Yet he would survive this chaos and degradation. What's more, while still a teenager, he would make headlines with a remarkable achievement.

Between the ages of seven and ten, Jamel was rarely in school. His mother sent him off to class each morning, but instead Jamel would go to the library.

At home, where he lived with his brother Eric and half-brother Chris, Jamel would hide in a closet to escape frequent fights between his mother and her new boyfriend. When there was no money for food, Jamel would sneak into school for the last serving of lunch and load his pockets with fruit and pastries for the family. At other times, they were reduced to panhandling.

Social workers wanted the children permanently removed from their mother's custody. One afternoon when Jamel was nine, a knock came to the door. Through the peephole, Jamel spied a social worker and two police officers. "Mom," he whispered, "it's the cops!"

His mother grabbed a roll of plastic garbage bags. "Throw your things in these!" As the police were forcing the door open, the family scrambled down the fire escape.

They spent a few nights in a city shelter, then moved into a single room in a seedy hotel in midtown Manhattan called the Prince George. It was crammed with the homeless and families on welfare. Drug dealers and prostitutes prowled the hallways. This training ground for crime would be Jamel's home for almost three years.

Pop! Pop! Pop! Jamel was startled from a fitful sleep. He recognized the sound of gunfire in the lobby.

Instead of investigating the commotion, Jamel reached for a book of poems by black writer Langston Hughes and tiptoed to the bathroom, which at least was quiet. He sat on the toilet and started reading.

What happens to a dream deferred?
Does it dry up
like a raisin in the sun?
Or fester like a sore—
And then run?

In the morning Jamel was found asleep in the bathroom, the book of poems still open on his lap.

"Give me your wallet." Ten-year-old Jamel stared fiercely into the eyes of a startled man he'd just stopped on the sidewalk. Seeing that the boy was unarmed, the man pushed him aside—only to have his path blocked by two older boys brandishing knives.

"*Give him the wallet,*" one boy snarled. The man meekly handed his money to Jamel.

This is easy, Jamel thought. *Why be poor?* Beginning with shoplifting for food, he had graduated to purse snatching, then muggings. But the streets had other lessons to teach.

"Here it is," Jamel panted triumphantly, running into the alley, holding up another wallet. He handed it to the team leader, Darrell.

"Uh huh." Darrell opened the wallet and found only a few singles and a ten. "What's this?" he hissed, waving the meager haul in Jamel's face. "You're holdin' out on us!"

Darrell pulled a gun and held it to Jamel's forehead. "Where's the rest?"

Jamel felt dizzy, paralyzed with fear. Then he heard himself blurting an improvised rap-style poem:

Head up or shut up.
I die, you cry,
Whatever forever.

Darrell blinked. Jamel repeated the poem, mantra-like, all the while stepping back. Finally, he turned and walked away, his father's voice echoing in his mind: *Keep using your head.*

"Hi!" he said, walking up to one of the drug dealers hanging out in front of the Prince George.

"Yeah, hi. Now beat it."

" 'What happens to a dream deferred?' "

The dealer frowned. "Say what? Look, kid, I'm busy. Don't be talkin' to me about no dreams."

" 'Does it dry up, like a raisin in the sun, or fester like a sore—and then run?' "

Jamel recited the entire poem to the astonished dealer, who reached into his pocket and peeled off a bill from a thick roll. "Here's ten. Go and remember-ize another poem."

Jamel became a lookout for the dealer, whom he knew only as Broderick. Now he had money for gold jewelry and designer clothes, and food for his family. He told his mother he was bagging groceries after school.

One afternoon when Jamel was eleven, he and Broderick were standing in the lobby of the Prince George, about to go shopping. Suddenly Jamel remembered something he'd left in the apartment. He stepped into the elevator. Just as the door closed and he started up, he heard pounding and Broderick's frantic voice.

"Jamel! Open up!"

Then he heard automatic gunfire, like a string of firecrackers, fading as he rose to safety.

Later, he took the elevator back down. Police had already covered Broderick's body with a bloodstained sheet. As Jamel watched, a painful memory welled up. *Another body being wheeled out*, he thought. *Just like my father.*

"Hey, Jamel." One of Broderick's teenage runners was poking him. "Did you see it? Cool!"

Jamel could only stare.

"Don't sweat it," said the runner. "We got work to do. There's a deal coming down."

Jamel tore his gold chain off his neck and thrust it in the older boy's face. "You only see the gold coming in. You don't see the bodies going out!" He threw down the chain and headed for the elevator. As he stepped inside, he thought he could hear his father's voice: *Use your head, son, use your head.* Then, with deliberation, Jamel pushed the UP button.

Over the next few months, Jamel steered clear of the drug dealers. He delivered groceries for extra cash, took control of the relief checks,

> *There is nothing on this earth more to be prized than good friendship.*
>
> THOMAS AQUINAS

paid bills. He got his brothers off to school and began attending regularly himself.

His grades picked up, and he joined every extracurricular group that would have him: a poetry club, a reading society, the Boy Scouts. His mother's condition improved, too, as a new medication cleared her mind. She applied for public housing, and the family settled into the Baruch Houses, a public project on the Lower East Side. Jamel, now twelve, felt for the first time that he had a grip on his life.

Then disaster struck again.

Two days before Thanksgiving, in 1989, Jeanne Oeser-Sweat suffered a complete breakdown. Chris and Eric were sent to foster homes, and Jamel was placed in a "transitional" home for 30 boys in Brooklyn.

The home was mostly for older boys, many of whom had criminal records, and they paid no attention to the wiry, bookish newcomer. Jamel struggled with depression. *I may be out of the Prince George, but I'm still in the ghetto,* he brooded. *"Use your head," Dad said. For what?*

Eventually, Jamel's mother was released, and the family regrouped in the projects. Able to concentrate on school again, the tenth-grader took a special liking to science and the tiny world of microorganisms, scoring a 99 on a final exam in biotechnology. But when Jeanne was again hospitalized later that year, Jamel's grades nose-dived and he started wisecracking teachers. He desperately needed someone to help him struggle out of the world of suspicion and foreboding now reflected in his poems:

Take a look at my life.
Where a man examines his life and
    lets out a sigh.
He knows there is one way out—
    that escape is to die.
Take a look at my life.

"In addition to identifying organisms through molecular diagnostic technology," said Edward J. Bottone, "we've got a method right here." With a dramatic flourish, he touched his nose. "To prove it to you, I'm going to identify these bacterial cultures with my eyes shut."

Bottone couldn't help noticing the fifteen-year-old boy, wearing a baseball cap turned backward, who was sitting at the far end of the big conference table. The young man was there along with 20 other inner-city students being recruited for the Secondary Education Through Health program. Jamel had been recommended for the program by his tenth-grade science teacher.

"Hmmm, this smells like grapes," Bottone continued, keeping his eyes closed and swirling a petri dish under his nostrils. "It's an opportunistic pathogen named *Pseudomonas aeruginosa.*"

As Bottone opened his eyes, the boy in the baseball cap blurted out, "That's all the guy does? *Smell* stuff?" The other students laughed.

Jamel had no idea he was insulting the director of consultative microbiology at New York's prestigious Mount Sinai Medical Center. And he certainly didn't think he'd be among the few selected for the program.

What neither Jamel nor Bottone knew then was that, along with an interest in science, they shared a similar upbringing. Bottone had grown up poor in a tough inner-city neighborhood—East Harlem. He, too, had floundered in early life. He understood the value of role models and heroes for kids struggling for a way out.

After he was accepted, Jamel reported to Mount Sinai to learn which staffer had been assigned to be his mentor. In walked Bottone. *Oh, no, not that weird guy who sniffs petri dishes!* Jamel turned and ran.

Halfway down the hall, Bottone caught up with him. "Hold on a minute," Bottone said, his arm over Jamel's shoulder as he led him toward the lab. "I need your help."

Jamel eyed the scientist warily. "What for?"

They now stood facing each other in the lab, with its rows of glass tubes and complicated-looking instruments. "We've got an interesting case here," Bottone continued. "A woman came to us with a skin infection called folliculitis. Now, the bug that caused this infection may only produce skin irritations—if the patient is healthy. But people with compromised immune systems, like AIDS patients, can die from it. We know it's pseudomonas. Smells like—"

"Yeah, I know. Smells like grapes."

"Right. And our patient has the same strain of pseudomonas we found in this." Bottone held up what looked like a Brillo pad.

"What's that?" asked Jamel.

"A loofah—a type of dried cucumber. People use them as beauty aids; they remove dead skin."

Bottone went on to explain that *Pseudomonas aeruginosa* grows naturally in almost any moist area, such as a swimming pool or bathroom. These sources usually don't transmit the bacteria to humans, but Bottone suspected that loofahs might.

Jamel went to work.

They looked to Jamel like thousands of wriggling pencils piled atop one another. In fact they were the offspring of a few pseudomonas cells he had injected into the loofah. "Hey, Doc," he called, lifting his head from the microscope, "check out the growth!" The potentially dangerous bacteria had exploded in the loofahs; the sponge was actually helping them grow.

Bottone peered into the instrument. "I see what you mean." He still couldn't get used to Jamel's knowing so much after having been with him only a few months.

Jamel watched, fascinated, as the bacteria writhed and pushed against one another. *Gotta respect the little buggers,* he thought. *Life is a struggle.*

A year later, Jamel was collecting data, testing different bacterial strains to see if the loofah supported their growth as well as that of *Pseudomonas aeruginosa.* Science had become a lightning rod for Jamel, directing and focusing his energies as nothing had before. Through countless hours in the hospital's library, he'd familiarized himself with more than 90 bacterial strains, tested them and carefully documented the results.

As his research expanded, Jamel shared his growing excitement by inviting friends into the project. They brought him used cosmetic aids like pumice stones, brushes and synthetic sponges. When he sampled the objects, he sometimes found pseudomonas. And the reason the objects were so dangerous became clear: when rubbed on the skin, they scratch open tiny routes to its interior.

How can we stop these buggers? Jamel wondered. He tried airdrying the sponges, but found it took months for pseudomonas to die out. Then he ran the objects through a washer and dryer. This killed pseudomonas but not other bacteria. Finally, after weeks of effort, he found the solution: he could stop *all* the bacteria in their tracks by soaking the objects in bleach. Through sheer perseverance, the boy from the projects had discovered a lethal weapon against what he called the "Rambo of pathogens."

"Budding Scientist's Success Breaks the Mold" ran the front-page headline in the New York *Times.* The news echoed in newspapers and medical journals around the world.

For his groundbreaking work with pseudomonas, Jamel had won first place in the prestigious New York City Science Fair and became the

My best friend is the man who in wishing me well wishes it for my sake.

ARISTOTLE

first student from Martin Luther King, Jr., High School to win the Westinghouse Science Talent Search. He is now a premed student at New York University.

Still, Jamel never forgets the lessons of his young life. When he received a community service award from the state bar association, a reporter asked him what all this prominence was like, considering his background.

"Well, you wear your suit and you go to these events, and then you have to be back in the projects by midnight," he said, a smile stealing over his face. "Just like Cinderella."

CALICO TALES

BY

PENNY PORTER

*T*hey stood on the edge of the desert, a small girl holding a kitten in her arms and an old rancher so tall and frail he swayed like a cypress in the wind.

"Boy calicos are scarce as hen's teeth," I heard him say. "Musta been that unusual blue fur that made him a boy!"

From the glint in the old man's eyes, I could tell he was a spinner of tall tales—and children are believers, because their world is still full of magic and miracles. I'd always heard, though, that because of a genetic abnormality, male calicos are very rare.

But this man could weave a spell, and I found myself believing him. A look at this very much alive kitten—and at the joy in my child's eyes—was all I needed to start doubting established fact.

Hugging the ball of fluff to her cheek, she said, "I'm going to name him Blueberry, Uncle Ralph, because blue's my favorite color."

"Mine too," he answered.

From the moment Jaymee and Ralph met several days before, there had been an immediate bonding of hearts. Our Arizona ranch was isolated among miles of yucca and mesquite beneath the vast blue sky, and now that her sister, Becky, had started school, our four-year-old felt small and alone.

Suddenly, the coughing of a distant motor announced the approach of an ancient pickup. The vehicle rolled into a barnyard pothole and rocked to a stop. "Mornin', ladies," the driver said as he pinched the brim of his hat. "I'm Ralph Cowan. Bill around?"

"He's in the horse barn," I said, conscious of Jaymee's arms locked around my knees.

My husband, Bill, had told me about Ralph Cowan, owner of the NI Ranch bordering ours. A well-known figure among cattlemen throughout the state, Ralph had once owned a spread so vast that it took 150 horses just to keep his ranch hands mounted. The father of three sons, he'd also found time to serve 14 years in the state legislature. But that had been decades before. Now, except for his niece Edythe, who took care of him, a few pets and his old horse, Dodger, Ralph was alone.

He opened the door and untangled his long legs, squaring his boots on the ground. He leaned forward and smiled at Jaymee. "I'll bet you like calico kittens," he said.

Jaymee's head bobbed.

"Well, I've got a brand-new litter at my place, and as soon as they're old enough, how 'bout I bring you one?"

Jaymee looked up at me. "I hope it's a boy, Mama," she murmured. "Daddy says no more girl cats!"

Ralph's blue eyes disappeared into a mask of friendly wrinkles. "Well, you tell your daddy if it's a boy, it's worth . . . five hundred dollars! That's more than he can get for a good yearling bull nowadays."

"Five hundred dollars!" Jaymee's eyes widened.

"Now, don't forget," Ralph cautioned, "a boy calico is hard to find. I've been lookin' for one most of my life. But we'll see if we can't find you one." As he smiled at Jaymee, a sudden warmth tugged at my heart.

"Yep," he continued, "a blue calico is as rare as a white tarantula."

"A white tarantula?" Jaymee squeezed me harder.

"They're out there somewhere," Ralph said. "You just gotta keep lookin'." I didn't think that white tarantulas existed, but who was I to break the spell that Ralph had woven.

During the weeks that followed, Ralph visited often to "talk cattle" with Bill. Sometimes, listing like a mast on a sinking schooner, he arrived on Dodger, his legs almost wrapped around the horse's middle. Most of the time he arrived in the truck. But it wasn't long before we realized it wasn't Bill he really came to see.

"Where's the little gal?" he'd ask.

Then came the day he brought Blueberry—pink nose, buttercup eyes, and frosted, silvery-blue fur. Ralph told Jaymee that Blueberry was a male. But it later dawned on me that he probably said this because he *wanted* it to be a male for Jaymee's sake. Jaymee arranged a box for the kitten on the back porch. There, he could come and go as he pleased at night, and light up her world by day.

Ralph, however, became the real flame for Jaymee. At the first sound of his pickup, she would cry, "Uncle Ralph's coming to play!" and dash to the end of our long driveway, Blueberry flailing like a mop in her arms. When they returned in Ralph's pickup, the calico would be reclining on the dashboard amid rusty spurs and fence pliers, while Ralph and Jaymee, seated on the worn seat cover, would be making plans. Soon they were searching for secrets among fallen cottonwoods and twisted mesquite and poking sticks into forbidden lairs.

"What do you and Uncle Ralph look for?" I asked Jaymee one afternoon.

"White tarantulas." She sighed heavily. "But we can't find any."

"What does Ralph say about that?"

"He says we gotta keep looking, because the only way you find things in life is by believing and looking."

One day she ran into the house, calling out "Mama! Chickies play songs before they hatch!"

I raised an eyebrow.

"Uncle Ralph took an egg out of the incubator and pressed it against his ear. Then he let me listen! He said it was tapping 'Yankee Doodle,' and I could hear it too."

One morning I caught the unlikely pair crouched conspiratorially over an anthill, heads nearly touching. "When ants build a hill around their house," Ralph began, "it means it's going to rain."

"Does Daddy know that?" Jaymee asked.

"Maybe not, sweetheart," he said, "but next time he goes out to bale hay, you check on the ants first. If they're buildin' a hill, tell him to wait a day." He winked at me.

Next to Becky, Ralph was Jaymee's best friend. But he was ill, and even at four, a child can worry. "He hurts, Mama," she said. "I can tell." To Becky she confided, "Uncle Ralph's going to be an angel soon. He told me so." *What'll happen when he's gone?* I wondered.

Meanwhile, Jaymee was absorbing his wisdom like alfalfa soaking up rain. From Ralph, she learned to whistle "Yankee Doodle." Hours and days of the same tune trying to be whistled can be nerve-shredding.

Then came the migration, a yearly event that prompts hundreds of huge, black, hairy tarantulas to cross sparsely traveled Route 666 in quest of mates. Ralph had planted the seed with Jaymee—and that's all it took.

"We have to go watch!" Jaymee insisted. "Maybe there'll be a white one!"

So off we went in the pickup: Becky, Jaymee, Blueberry and I, with a coffee can to put "Whitey" in. Parked on the side of the road, we watched the phenomenon as Becky counted, ". . . 307 . . . 308 . . . 309 . . ." and Jaymee kept "almost" seeing a white one. I prayed there was no such creature, knowing in my heart that nothing would make me get out of that truck to catch one. Thankfully, I was spared.

Then the monsoon season arrived, bringing torrential storms, and toads and frogs by the thousands. Puddles simmered with tadpoles—and then, gradually, the water began drying up. "The polliwogs are dying, Uncle Ralph," Jaymee said, full of sadness.

"Can't let that happen," he said. "There'd be nothing around to catch the mosquitoes—and we'd be eaten alive!" For the rest of the day, Jaymee scurried back and forth with coffee cans of water to keep the puddles full.

Why, I wondered, did Ralph spend so much time with Jaymee? The day she found an old box turtle living under the log pile offered a clue. "I'm going to feed him lettuce every day," she told Ralph.

"I'll bet he'd like Oreo cookies better," Ralph said as he leaned down to pick up the turtle. He paused—then ran his stiff fingers over worn letters carved on its ancient shell. "RC," he whispered softly.

Of course! I thought. *Ralph Cowan.* Had he been the one to carve these initials years and years before? But the storyteller soon rearranged my thinking.

"His name was . . . Running Coyote," Ralph began, his eyes misting. "He was an old Indian friend of mine. He had a little girl just like you." He looked at Jaymee. "And he carved these initials into this shell some 50 years ago—just for her. He loved her very much."

Running Coyote? Ralph Cowan?

My heart softened. Was this another tall tale? *But what does it matter?* I thought. The important thing was that he had awakened in Jaymee a curiosity and love for the world around her, and in her bright-eyed innocence and enthusiasm, she had touched his heart and brought him back to the wonders of life. And yet, I couldn't help thinking about those initials.

How rare and wonderful is that flash of a moment when we realize we have discovered a friend.

WILLIAM ROTSLER

164

Ralph's visits suddenly stopped. A phone call from Edythe confirmed our fears. He was laid up—badly injured by a bull. "It'll be a while before he can drive again," she said.

When we arrived at the NI to visit Ralph, he was sitting on the porch steps patting a dog so old that not even a thump was left in its tail.

"Why did the bull hurt you, Uncle Ralph?" Jaymee asked.

As frail as the storyteller was, he still spun his magic. "He's old, sweetheart," Ralph said, "and his skull's getting so thick, it's squeezing his brain. It hurts. So he got mean." Jaymee nodded sadly and put Blueberry on Ralph's lap, while I went inside to talk with Edythe.

We could see the two through the kitchen window, talking quietly. "Wouldn't you love to hear that conversation?" I said.

Edythe smiled. "Ralph has always loved children. Did you know he lost his own little girl when she was about Jaymee's age? Her name was Ruth . . ."

Ruth Cowan. RC. Suddenly, my mind filled with the vision of a young father scratching those initials on a box turtle for a very small girl. And just as suddenly, I knew that it was one of life's eerie quirks of timing that had brought Ralph and Jaymee together at a moment when they were both lonely and needed a kindred spirit.

Heading home, I noticed Jaymee squeezing Blueberry much too tightly. A tiny furrow creased her forehead. "What's wrong, honey?" I asked.

"Uncle Ralph told me . . . Blueberry's going to have . . . babies!" she said, her lip trembling. "Uncle Ralph says it's a miracle, Mama . . . and since only God makes mistakes, to tell Daddy that Blueberry's worth a lot more than $500."

"Of course he is, honey." I hugged her close.

When Becky started school again, Jaymee didn't seem so alone anymore. She spent hours feeding cookies to RC and searching for white tarantulas. Soon she was caring for the "boy" calico's nine "miracle kittens."

The next time we visited the NI Ranch, Ralph sat huddled in an ancient leather chair, a wool blanket around his shoulders. He smiled and talked with Jaymee and Becky. When we got up to leave, he insisted on seeing us to the door.

"Did I ever show you my cattle brand?" he asked the girls, pointing to an empty hole in the living room ceiling. "There used to be a neon light hanging there, molded into the letters NI." His hand trembled as it covered the wall switch. "I lit it every night," he said, "a long time ago." His eyes sought Jaymee's. "It was blue," he murmured, "just as blue as your calico."

Uncle Ralph disappeared from her life as quietly as he'd entered it, dying peacefully in his sleep. Years passed before we witnessed the absolute power of his storytelling.

Almost everything a child hears and sees is tucked away for remembering. Later it can resurface exactly as it really was—or as the heart wants it to be.

Jaymee and Becky were in their teens, and Bill had just rewired the wagon-wheel chandelier he had made for me years before. This time he added seven blinding-white light bulbs. "Gosh, Daddy," Becky said. "You'd better invest in a dimmer switch. That's so bright, it's like hanging the sun in the house." She turned to Jaymee. "Don't you think so?"

But Jaymee's thoughts were elsewhere. Smiling, she wrapped her arms about her knees as though hugging the memory that came drifting back. "Do you remember Uncle Ralph's chandelier, Beck?" Jaymee asked. "The one with the NI brand on his living-room ceiling?"

Becky looked puzzled. "No . . ."

"Well, I do." Jaymee's brown eyes shone. "When Uncle Ralph clicked the switch, it glowed—the prettiest and richest shade of blue I ever saw—just like my blue calico. I remember it."

And I knew she always would.

A friend is someone you can do nothing

with, and enjoy it.

THE OPTIMIST MAGAZINE

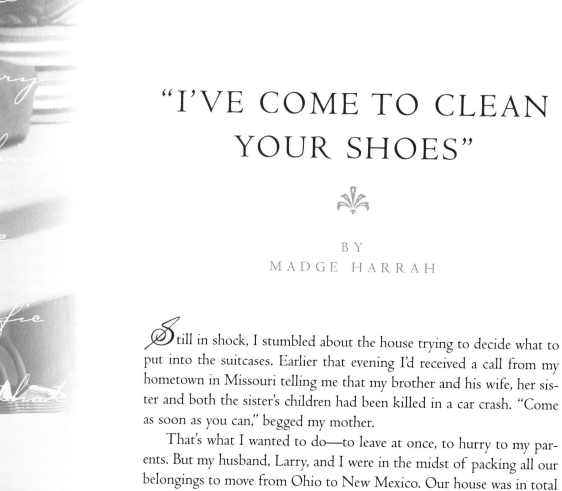

"I'VE COME TO CLEAN YOUR SHOES"

BY

MADGE HARRAH

*S*till in shock, I stumbled about the house trying to decide what to put into the suitcases. Earlier that evening I'd received a call from my hometown in Missouri telling me that my brother and his wife, her sister and both the sister's children had been killed in a car crash. "Come as soon as you can," begged my mother.

That's what I wanted to do—to leave at once, to hurry to my parents. But my husband, Larry, and I were in the midst of packing all our belongings to move from Ohio to New Mexico. Our house was in total confusion. Some of the clothes that Larry and I and our two young children, Eric and Meghan, would need were already taped up in cartons. Which ones? Stunned by grief, I couldn't remember. Other clothes lay unwashed in a pile on the laundry-room floor. Supper dishes still sat on the kitchen table. Toys were strewn everywhere.

While Larry made plane reservations for the following morning, I wandered about the house, aimlessly picking things up and putting them down. I couldn't focus. Again and again, the words I'd heard on the phone echoed through my head: "Bill is gone—Marilyn too. June—and both the children . . ."

It was as though the message had muffled my brain with cotton. Whenever Larry spoke, he sounded far away. As I moved through the house, I ran into doors and tripped over chairs.

Larry made arrangements for us to leave by seven o'clock the next morning. Then he phoned a few friends to tell them what had happened. Occasionally, someone asked to speak to me. "If there's anything I can do, let me know," that person would offer kindly.

"Thank you very much," I'd reply. But I didn't know what to ask for. I couldn't concentrate.

I sat in a chair, staring into space, while Larry called Donna King, the woman with whom I taught a nursery class at church each Sunday. Donna and I were casual friends, but we didn't see each other often. She and Emerson, her thin, quiet husband, were kept busy during the weekdays by their own "nursery"—six children ranging in age from two years to fifteen. I was glad Larry had thought to warn her that she'd have the nursery class alone the coming Sunday.

While I sat there, Meghan darted by, clutching a ball. Eric chased after her. *They should be in bed,* I thought. I followed them into the living room. My legs dragged. My hands felt gloved with lead. I sank down on the couch in a stupor.

When the doorbell rang, I rose slowly and crept across the room. I opened the door to see Emerson King standing on the porch.

"I've come to clean your shoes," he said.

Confused, I asked him to repeat.

"Donna had to stay with the baby," he said, "but we want to help you. I remember when my father died, it took me hours to get the children's shoes cleaned and shined for the funeral. So that's what I've come to do for you. Give me all your shoes—not just your good shoes, but *all* your shoes."

I hadn't even thought about shoes until he mentioned them. Now I remembered that Eric had left the sidewalk to wade through the mud in his good shoes after church the previous Sunday. Not to be outdone by her brother, Meghan had kicked rocks, scuffing the toes of her shoes. When we returned, I'd tossed them into the laundry room, for cleaning sometime later.

While Emerson spread newspapers on the kitchen floor, I gathered Larry's dress and everyday shoes, my heels, my flats, the children's dirty dress shoes and their sneakers with the food spots. Emerson found a pan that he filled with soapy water. He got an old knife out of a drawer and retrieved a sponge from under the sink. Larry had to rummage through several cartons, but at last he located the shoe polish.

Emerson settled himself on the floor and got to work. Watching him concentrate intently on one task helped me pull my own thoughts into order. *Laundry first,* I told myself. While the washer chugged, Larry and I bathed the children and put them to bed.

While we cleared the supper dishes, Emerson continued to work, saying nothing. I thought of Jesus washing the feet of his disciples. Our Lord had knelt, serving his friends, even as this man now knelt, serving us. The love in that act released my tears at last, healing rain to wash the fog from my mind. I could move. I could think. I could get on with the business of living.

One by one, the jobs fell into place. I went into the laundry room to put a load of wash into the dryer, returning to the kitchen to find that Emerson had left. In a line against one wall stood all our shoes, gleaming, spotless. Later, when I started to pack, I saw that Emerson had even scrubbed the soles. I could put the shoes directly into the suitcases.

We got to bed late and rose very early, but by the time we left for the airport, all the jobs were done. Ahead lay grim, sad days, but the comfort of Christ's presence, symbolized by the image of a quiet man kneeling on my kitchen floor with a pan of water, would sustain me.

Now, whenever I hear of an acquaintance who has lost a loved one, I no longer call with the vague offer, "If there's anything I can do . . ." Now I try to think of one specific task that suits that person's need— such as washing the family car, taking their dog to the boarding kennel, or house-sitting during the funeral. And if the person says to me, "How did you know I needed that done?" I reply, "It's because a man once cleaned my shoes."

THE STRANGER WHO TAUGHT MAGIC

BY

ARTHUR GORDON

That July morning, I remember, was like any other, calm and opalescent before the heat of the fierce Georgia sun. I was thirteen: sunburned, shaggy-haired, a little aloof, and solitary. In winter I had to put on shoes and go to school like everyone else. But summers I lived by the sea, and my mind was empty and wild and free.

On this particular morning, I had tied my rowboat to the pilings of an old dock upriver from our village. There, sometimes, the striped sheepshead lurked in the still, green water. I was crouched, motionless as a stone, when a voice spoke suddenly above my head: "Canst thou draw out leviathan with a hook, or his tongue with a cord which thou lettest down?"

I looked up, startled, into a lean, pale face and a pair of the most remarkable eyes I had ever seen. It wasn't a question of color; I'm not sure, now, what color they were. It was a combination of things: warmth, humor, interest, alertness. Intensity—that's the word, I guess—and, underlying it all, a curious kind of mocking sadness. I believe I thought him old.

He saw how taken aback I was. "Sorry," he said. "It's a bit early in the morning for the Book of Job, isn't it?" He nodded at the two or three fish in the boat. "Think you could teach me how to catch those?"

Ordinarily, I was wary of strangers, but anyone interested in fishing was hardly a stranger. I nodded, and he climbed down into the boat. "Perhaps we should introduce ourselves," he said. "But then again, perhaps not. You're a boy willing to teach, I'm a teacher willing to learn. That's introduction enough. I'll call you 'Boy,' and you call me 'Sir.' "

Such talk sounded strange in my world of sun and salt water. But there was something so magnetic about the man, and so disarming about his smile, that I didn't care.

I handed him a hand line and showed him how to bait his hooks with fiddler crabs. He kept losing baits, because he could not recognize a sheepshead's stealthy tug, but he seemed content not to catch anything. He told me he had rented one of the weathered bungalows behind the dock. "I needed to hide for a while," he said. "Not from the police, or anything like that. Just from friends and relatives. So don't tell anyone you've found me, will you?"

I was tempted to ask where he was from; there was a crispness in the way he spoke that was very different from the soft accents I was accustomed to. But I didn't. He had said he was a teacher, though, and so I asked what he taught.

"In the school catalogue they call it English," he said. "But I like to think of it as a course in magic—in the mystery and magic of words. Are you fond of words?"

I said that I had never thought much about them. I also pointed out that the tide was ebbing, that the current was too strong for more fishing, and that in any case it was time for breakfast.

"Of course," he said, pulling in his line. "I'm a little forgetful about such things these days." He eased himself back onto the dock with a little grimace, as if the effort cost him something. "Will you be back on the river later?"

I said that I would probably go casting for shrimp at low tide.

"Stop by," he said. "We'll talk about words for a while, and then perhaps you can show me how to catch shrimp."

So began a most unlikely friendship, because I did go back. To this day, I'm not sure why. Perhaps it was because, for the first time, I had met an adult on terms that were in balance. In the realm of words and ideas, he might be the teacher. But in my own small universe of winds and tides and sea creatures, the wisdom belonged to me.

Almost every day after that, we'd go wherever the sea gods or my whim decreed. Sometimes up the silver creeks, where the terrapin skittered down the banks and the great blue herons stood like statues. Sometimes along the ocean dunes, fringed with graceful sea oats, where by night the great sea turtles crawled and by day the wild goats browsed. I showed him where the mullet swirled and where the flounder lay in cunning camouflage. I learned that he was incapable of much exertion; even pulling up the anchor seemed to exhaust him. But he never complained. And, all the time, talk flowed from him like a river.

Much of it I have forgotten now, but some comes back as clear and distinct as if it all happened yesterday, not decades ago. We might be sitting in a hollow of the dunes, watching the sun go down in a smear of crimson. "Words," he'd say. "Just little black marks on paper. Just sounds in the empty air. But think of the power they have! They can make you laugh or cry, love or hate, fight or run away. They can heal or hurt. They even come to look and sound like what they mean. Angry *looks* angry on the page. Ugly *sounds* ugly when you say it. Here!" He would hand me a piece of shell. "Write a word that looks or sounds like what it means."

I would stare helplessly at the sand.

"Oh," he'd cry, "you're being dense. There are so many! Like whisper . . . leaden . . . twilight . . . chime. Tell you what: when you go to bed tonight, think of five words that look like what they mean and five that sound like what they mean. Don't go to sleep until you do!"

And I would try—but always fall asleep.

Or we might be anchored just offshore, casting into the surf for sea bass, our little bateau nosing over the rollers like a restless hound. "Rhythm," he would say. "Life is full of it; words should have it, too. But you have to train your ear. Listen to the waves on a quiet night; you'll pick up the cadence. Look at the patterns the wind makes in dry sand and you'll see how syllables in a sentence should fall. Do you know what I mean?"

My conscious self didn't know; but perhaps something deep inside me did. In any case, I listened.

I listened, too, when he read from the books he sometimes brought: Kipling, Conan Doyle, Tennyson's *Idylls of the King*. Often he would stop and repeat a phrase or a line that pleased him. One day, in Malory's *Le Morte d'Arthur*, he found one: "And the great horse grimly neighed." "Close your eyes," he said to me, "and say that slowly, out loud." I did. "How did it make you feel?" "It gives me the shivers," I said truthfully. He was delighted.

But the magic that he taught was not confined to words; he had a way of generating in me an excitement about things I had always taken for granted. He might point to a bank of clouds. "What do you see there? Colors? That's not enough. Look for towers and drawbridges. Look for dragons and griffins and strange and wonderful beasts."

Or he might pick up an angry, claw-brandishing blue crab, holding it cautiously by the back flippers as I had taught him. "Pretend you're this crab," he'd say. "What do you see through those stalk-like eyes? What do you feel with those complicated legs? What goes on in your tiny brain? Try it for just five seconds. Stop being a boy. Be a crab!" And

I would stare in amazement at the furious creature, feeling my comfortable identity lurch and sway under the impact of the idea.

So the days went by. Our excursions became less frequent, because he tired so easily. He brought two chairs down to the dock and some books, but he didn't read much. He seemed content to watch me as I fished, or the circling gulls, or the slow river coiling past.

A sudden shadow fell across my life when my parents told me I was going to camp for two weeks. On the dock that afternoon I asked my friend if he would be there when I got back. "I hope so," he said gently.

But he wasn't. I remember standing on the sun-warmed planking of the old dock, staring at the shuttered bungalow and feeling a hollow sense of finality and loss. I ran to Jackson's grocery store—where everyone knew everything—and asked where the schoolteacher had gone.

"He was sick, real sick," Mrs. Jackson replied. "Doc phoned his relatives up north to come get him. He left something for you—he figured you'd be asking after him."

She handed me a book. It was a slender volume of verse, *Flame and Shadow*, by someone I had never heard of: Sara Teasdale. The corner of one page was turned down, and there was a penciled star by one of the poems. I still have the book, with that poem, "On the Dunes."

A friend is one before whom

I may think aloud.

RALPH WALDO EMERSON

> *If there is any life when death is*
>   *over,*
> *These tawny beaches will know*
>   *much of me,*
> *I shall come back, as constant and*
>   *as changeful*

176

As the unchanging, many-colored
    sea.
If life was small, if it has made me
    scornful,
Forgive me; I shall straighten
    like a flame
In the great calm of death, and if
    you want me
Stand on the sea-ward dunes and
    call my name.

Well, I have never stood on the dunes and called his name. For one thing, I never knew it; for another, I'd be too self-conscious. And there are long stretches when I forget all about him. But sometimes—when the music or the magic in a phrase makes my skin tingle, or when I pick up an angry blue crab, or when I see a dragon in the flaming sky—sometimes I remember.

A KINDNESS RETURNED

BY

VIRGINIA HALL GRAVES

At the time my son was born in 1956, I shared a hospital room with a young woman who bore a son on the same day. Partly because my parents owned a florist shop, the room was soon filled with the lovely scent of roses.

As the seventh floral arrangement was brought in, I was beginning to feel uncomfortable, for no flowers had arrived for my roommate, Ann. She sat on the edge of her bed and leaned forward to admire the latest bouquet. She was a pretty young woman, yet there was something about her large, brown eyes that made me think she had known too much struggling, too much sadness for one so young. I had the feeling she had always had to admire someone else's flowers.

"I'm enjoying every minute of this," she said as though she had read my thoughts and was trying to reassure me. "Wasn't I the lucky one to get you for a roommate?"

I still felt uncomfortable, however. If only there were some magic button I could push to take away the sadness in her eyes. *Well,* I thought, *at least I can see that she has some flowers.* When my mother and father came to see me that day, I asked them to send her some.

The flowers arrived just as Ann and I were finishing supper.

"Another bouquet for you," she said, laughing.

"No, not this time," I said, looking at the card. "These are for you."

Ann stared at the blossoms a long time, not saying anything. She ran her fingers across the pale-blue ceramic bootee and lightly touched each of the sweetheart roses nestled inside as though trying to engrave them on her memory.

"How can I ever thank you?" she said softly when she finally spoke.

I was almost embarrassed. It was such a little kindness on my part.

The son born to my husband and me that day in 1956 turned out to be our only child. For nearly 21 years he filled our lives with love and laughter, making us feel complete. But on Easter morning in April 1977, after a long, painful battle with cancer, he died quietly in our arms.

At the funeral home I was alone with my son in a room filled with the scent of roses, when a deliveryman brought in a tiny bouquet. I didn't read the card until later, as we rode to the cemetery. "To W. John Graves," the card said, "from the boy who was born with you at Memorial Hospital, and his mother."

Only then did I recognize the ceramic bootee I had given to a sad young woman so many years ago, now once again filled with roses. Ann and I had long since lost touch. She had never known our son, never been aware of his illness. She must have read his obituary in a newspaper. I passed the card on to my mother sitting beside me. She, too, remembered.

"A kindness returned," Mother said.

A few days later, my husband and I, with several members of our family, went to the cemetery to clear John's grave. The bootee of roses sat at its foot, towered over by tall wreaths and sprays.

"How odd that anyone would send something like that to a funeral," someone said. "It seems more appropriate for a birth."

"There *was* a birth," said my husband quietly. "John was born into Eternal Life." I looked at him with surprise, knowing those words were difficult for a man who had never spoken openly about such matters.

He emptied out the flowers and handed me the ceramic bootee. I held it and, just as Ann had done, I traced it with my fingers, thinking of all the messages it contained: the embers of friendship that glow through the years, gratitude remembered and, beneath it all, the promise of Resurrection, which comforts us now.

True friendship is like phosphorescence—
it glows best when the world around you
goes dark.

DENISE MARTIN

MY UNFORGETTABLE "ANIMAL LADY"

BY
BOB NOONAN

"Maybe it's a rattlesnake!" I said. Dad and I looked into the big metal milk can at the three-foot-long spotted snake. I was eight, and we had just moved to rural Scarborough, Maine. I discovered the snake in a quarry near the house, grabbed it behind the head like the professional snake handlers I'd read about, and carried it home.

We showed it to a neighbor. "Can't tell you what it is," he said, "but Helen Perley can. The Animal Lady who runs White Animal Farm. Lives about a mile from here."

Dad drove the snake and me down the hill on Seavey Landing Road and stopped the car beside a thicket of evergreens and lilacs. A gate was hidden in the greenery. Beyond it was a yard, bordered by a house and two other buildings, about 30 feet across and cluttered with homemade wooden cages.

We passed through the gate into another world, which exploded into life. Rabbits bolted across the lawn, zigzagging frantically away. Pigeons lifted from the roofs in a clatter of multicolored wings. A raccoon, its nose against the wire of its cage, poked its fingers inquisitively through.

Two white ducks waddled by, and a huge peacock rushed to the center of the yard and stared belligerently at us. Dad and I stood openmouthed.

The screen door on the main building sprang open, and a short, slender woman appeared. "I'm Helen," she said, shaking hands with us. She wore a blue turtleneck jersey, blue jeans and brown work boots. A hammer hung from her belt. Her short brown hair was curled in a puffy bouffant hairdo.

After Dad explained our visit, she reached into the milk can and picked the snake up. The snake wrapped itself around her arm, twisting and turning. She caressed the creature gently, and it stopped struggling.

"It's harmless," she said. "Just a milk snake. It's a beautiful specimen. Are you the snake hunter?" Her clear blue eyes looked into mine, and I nodded with pride.

"Would you like to hunt snakes for me? I'll teach you how." *Would I!* It was 1952, and my heroes were Arctic explorers, wild-animal trainers and the crew of the *Kon-Tiki*. On the spot, I belonged to Helen.

Dad and I got the grand tour. We met golden and silver pheasants, the raccoon and a coati-mundi, an oddly shaped animal the size of a small dog. We watched turtles swimming in an old Victorian bathtub. Pointing to an enormous lump of white bone, six feet long and with eye sockets big enough to sit in, Helen said somberly, "Sea monster skull." My eyes widened. Later she confessed it was a whale skull.

She took us inside the main building. The aisles were lined with cages full of mice, rats, gerbils and hamsters. There were also exotic pets, reptiles and a variety of other wild animals. The entire building chirped, whistled, screeched, squeaked and rustled with life.

With all the animal chores and the constant flow of visitors, she and her husband, Paul, a big, quiet man in overalls and feed cap, were almost always working. Helen's animal business had started 20 years earlier when she brought home a pair of white rats for her young children, Jack and June. The rats started to multiply, Helen built more cages, and

White Animal Farm was born. Although her formal training ended at high school, her lifelong education in animal husbandry had begun.

She started my reptile education at the boa constrictor cage. After showing me how to hold snakes without hurting them, she handed me live specimens of the local species she sought. I went home profoundly excited. I wanted to be like Helen Perley when I grew up.

I made a snake bag out of a pillowcase, as Helen had instructed. I looked where she said to look: under rocks and boards and tarpaper, along paths and in fields. I walked the way she told me to, treading slowly and lightly to avoid the vibrations that alarm small animals. And I discovered much more than snakes. I found spiderwebs, bird nests, wildflowers, anthills, unusual rocks, eggshells and bizarre insects. Each discovery fed my curiosity.

Every few days I coasted down the hill to Helen's on my bike, the pillowcase full of everything I'd found tied to the handlebars. Helen would put down her work, buy the snakes, identify everything else and answer all my questions.

For six summers I biked to Helen's at least once a week. The second year, I shyly showed her my animal drawings. She liked my work, and that gave me immense confidence.

When I was ten, I discovered taxidermy. Helen gave me a dead pigeon for my first attempt. As I handed her the finished specimen, a bulging caricature of the original bird, she nodded approval and I knew I was a success.

Another time she raised her head at a commotion of wings outside and motioned me to follow her. We watched a flock of her pigeons fleeing across a marsh, a hawk in pursuit. The hawk scattered the birds, then flew straight up. The pigeons regrouped and flapped vigorously back toward us. One white bird lagged behind. Suddenly the hawk began to fall, twisting down so fast I could barely follow its movement. It hit the lagging pigeon in an explosion of white feathers, driving it almost to the marsh. Then, clutching the limp white bundle, the hawk flapped slowly toward some tall pines.

It was the most dramatic sight of my young life, and I understood suddenly that life and death are coworkers. As Helen had told me, some things have to die so others can live.

Helen was the most real person I ever met. She loved what she was doing so completely, there was no need to pretend to be anyone else. A young boy grasps those lessons quickly: Do what you love. Respect life.

Everybody in Scarborough knew Helen, and there were endless stories about her. One night a hysterical neighbor called. "Helen! There's a snake in my kitchen window!" Helen rushed over and found a four-foot boa constrictor curled up on the outside windowsill. "It's Beauregard!" she said. "He's been gone for two weeks."

Another woman, who found a snake in her Christmas tree, started a petition demanding that Helen get rid of her snakes. No one would sign it; people liked Helen. Besides, Mainers love a good story, and there was no way they'd cramp the style of anyone who supplied as many as Helen did. Helen had a great sense of humor. If visitors were neophytes, she would show them the stiff tails of the fantail pigeons and inform them, "I starch the tails myself." If they accepted that, they were next taken to the golden pheasants, and Helen would say, "I painted the birds myself." Sometimes people would ask how she did it, and she'd launch into a discussion on bird painting.

She slipped duck eggs under rabbits and told people they were rabbit eggs. Sometimes she had rabbits nursing orphaned kittens, or cats nursing orphaned rabbits. "First successful crossbreeding of the cat and the rabbit," she'd solemnly announce. "The cabit." But she'd always give herself away with a smile and admit the truth.

Helen was probably best known in Scarborough as a healer of animals. Over the years a parade of wounded birds and animals, brought to her by the public, passed through her hands. Once I brought her a chipmunk with a wound on its stomach. Helen reached into the live trap and gently gripped the little animal. I knew from experience that chipmunks bite, but this one lay passive and trusting as Helen held it belly up and cleaned the wound. The next day it was bright-eyed and active, its tail jauntily erect.

Pet-shop professionals from across the country called Helen for advice on diet, disease, breeding and training. She sold chipmunks to Dawn Animal Agency for films, and provided numerous laboratories with animals for research. At its peak, White Animal Farm had over 33,000 animals, mostly laboratory rats and mice. They were in great demand by universities, hospitals and government laboratories because of their health and the purity of their breeds, several of which Helen herself had developed.

First and last, though, Helen was a teacher. She gave innumerable tours through the farm and nature walks in the woods. She took animals to schools and nursing homes. If a young person had a special passion for animals, Helen spotted it instantly, calling it "the spark." She gave that youngster personal attention and encouraged him to come back.

When I was fourteen my parents bought a farm 50 miles away. Sad about the move, I bicycled down the hill to Helen's. "You'll love Windham," she said. "Wonderful farm country with lots of new wildlife." With those words of affirmation, she set me free.

Years passed. I left Maine and returned. Then in my early forties, both my marriage and career as a builder ended. I was adrift. For years I'd been selling a few wildlife articles and drawings, and the idea of doing it for a living excited me. But I was full of fear and indecision. Then I thought about Helen. She knew exactly what to do with her life. *Teach people about animals. Do what you love.* So I decided to concentrate on writing about wildlife. I've been doing it ever since.

My nephew is a wildlife fanatic like me. In 1991, when he was eight, I took Kyle to meet Helen.

The buildings were sagging more than I remembered. There were empty cages. But the screen door to the main building sprang open, and a tiny woman in a blue turtleneck and jeans appeared. A hammer hung on her belt. Friendly blue eyes looked at us from the lined face as I made the introductions. Kyle asked Helen a question about feeding his hamster, and they were soon deep in conversation. Helen had seen the spark.

We got the tour, Kyle asking questions constantly, Helen answering in detail. "Here's a sea monster skull," she told us. While she showed him around, I went inside the main building. A boy about twelve was cleaning cages.

"Working for Helen?" I asked. He nodded.

"You like it?"

He gave me a look as if to say, Like it? What a question! I love it!

My heart filled; all of us kids, across all those years. I wanted to say something, but I couldn't find the words. Then Kyle called out, "Uncle Bob! A boa constrictor!" I rejoined Helen's tour. On the ride home Kyle talked about the farm nonstop. "I want to be Helen Perley when I grow up," he said.

Helen's heart gave out in October 1994. She was ninety. I think of her often. And I remember that, thanks to her, I'm doing what I love.

ONE THOUSAND MEN
AND A BABY

BY

LAWRENCE ELLIOTT

One lonely Saturday night in July 1953, a medical orderly at an Army dispensary in war-devastated Korea went out to have a smoke and kicked a bundle of newspapers out of his way. A feeble little cry shivered up from the darkness.

It was a child—a gasping, emaciated infant.

Soon the orderly was racing toward the Star of the Sea Children's Home in Inchon. There he handed the bundle to a nun who unwrapped the scrawny little body. The baby was a boy, perhaps a month old. And his eyes were blue.

The war was entering its fourth year. Inchon had been overrun, liberated, shelled and starved, and the Star of the Sea orphanage had been spared little. Staffed by overworked French nuns and a dozen Korean aides, it was run by Sister Philomena, a crafty, tough-minded Irish nurse.

Her orphanage was so desperately overburdened that when the children became teenagers they had to be sent out on their own. There was never enough food or clothing. *What would she do with this half-Caucasian baby?* she wondered.

Sister knew in her heart that there could never be a place here for a blue-eyed child. He would always be scorned as "the white one." When her back was turned, the Korean aides ignored the baby. Even if he somehow managed to grow to adulthood, she realized, he would be a pariah—despised and harassed as the abandoned offspring of an American soldier.

So when the U.S.S. *Point Cruz*—as escort carrier that had been in the thick of the action—dropped anchor in Inchon harbor early in September, Sister Philomena had an idea. She sent a message to the chaplain, Lieutenant Edward O. Riley.

They were old friends. Sometimes, with the connivance of the *Point Cruz*'s captain, Father Riley brought the children things from the ship's stores: powdered milk, cough medicine, aspirin. When he arrived at the orphanage, Sister Philomena told him about the baby the orderly had brought her from ASCOM—the U.S. Army Service Command headquarters. Then she took him to the nursery.

Blue eyes stared up at them. The infant was all ribs and swollen abdomen. A rash covered his face. "I haven't proper medicine or food," Sister Philomena said. "Surely you can do something, Father. After all, he's an American."

Father Riley brooded about it, then went to talk to his skipper.

"Does this baby have a name?" the skipper asked.

"George—after the orderly who brought him in," said the chaplain.

"What are the chances he might be adopted by a Korean family?"

"Zero."

"Then here's what I want you to do," said Captain John T. Hayward, nicknamed Chick, who had once been expelled from a military academy, never finished high school, and thus knew something about starting out against the odds. "Find some Korean official who will issue this kid a passport. But first we're going to bring him aboard the *Point Cruz* and keep him here until he's healthy."

Father Riley was elated. But he felt obliged to ask how the Navy would take to the idea of housing an infant aboard an aircraft carrier.

"Hayward's Law," came the crisp reply, "holds that, in an emergency, regulations are to be intelligently disregarded."

"God bless you," said the chaplain gruffly, and went off to battle the Korean bureaucracy.

A week later he was back, sagging with discouragement. He had trudged all over Inchon and beseeched countless government functionaries. But no birth certificate—no passport.

Chick Hayward didn't flinch. "I guess we have to go right to the top." Taking a bottle of whiskey out of his safe, he said, "Father, this is my last bottle. Maybe you'll find someone in the foreign ministry in Seoul who needs it more than we do. Don't come back without the passport."

The hospital ship U.S.S. *Consolation* had been in port three weeks before Lieutenant Hugh Keenan, a surgeon from Spokane, Washington, set foot on land. It was a blazing-hot September morning, and his two companions, old hands in Inchon, suggested visiting the Star of the Sea orphanage. "We can get out of the sun and Sister Philomena will give us tea."

But Sister had more than tea on her agenda. She fixed a canny eye on the newcomer and, having ascertained that he was married and had an eight-year-old daughter, led him to the nursery. When Keenan came back he was holding a rashy, blue-eyed baby. "Here," Sister Philomena said, producing a bottle, "you feed him."

Holding the child eased an ache the surgeon had carried a long time. He and his wife had lost several babies during their marriage—the last one, a boy, about a year before. Now, leaving, he promised, "I'll bring something for that rash."

He was back the next day with ointment. Then he sat down and began feeding baby George. "Tell me, doctor," Sister Philomena asked, "is it likely that you might want to adopt a little tyke like this one?"

"Yes, it's likely," Keenan said.

When he returned to the *Consolation,* he asked for his captain's advice.

"Lieutenant, your job is to take care of military personnel," the captain said. Keenan had to tell Sister Philomena that adopting George was out of the question. But he kept coming back to hold the baby.

Then came a long stretch when he couldn't get shore leave. When he finally got back to the orphanage Sister told him George was gone. Her friend, Chaplain Edward Riley, had received a passport for him and taken him to the *Point Cruz.* "He's going to send George to an orphanage in America."

"The hell he is!" Keenan yelled as he ran out.

When Father Riley carried "George Cruz Ascom" up the gangway of the *Point Cruz,* 1000 men lined the rail. For days, they had worked to prepare a nursery in the sick bay. Ship's carpenters had built a crib and playpen. Both were so full of homemade rattles and toys that there was barely room for George. A foot-high stack of diapers had been cut from Navy sheets and painstakingly hemmed in the ship's laundry.

The baby was put in the charge of two hospital corpsmen, both seasoned fathers. The flight surgeon, a pediatrician in civilian life, had the galley make special formula. Within days the listless, spindly infant began filling out and worming around in his crib.

So many men requested permission to visit the nursery that Captain Hayward instituted "Baby-san Call." After nap time each afternoon, the ship's public-address system would blare out: "Attention all hands! Baby-san on the hangar deck from 1400 hours!" Men would run for their cameras and file past the bomb cart that had become a baby carriage. They would coo at George and snap his picture. Some offered George a forefinger and he would curl his tiny fist around it and laugh.

One loyal friend is worth ten thousand relatives.

EURIPIDES

191

"That baby had one thousand uncles," said William J. Powers, the petty officer in charge of the hangar deck. "By then, the armistice was signed and we were all waiting to go home, and along comes this little kid to hit us right in the heart. It was as though he was the peace we'd been fighting for."

George had been aboard the *Point Cruz* more than a week the day Lieutenant Hugh Keenan came stomping up the gangway looking for Father Riley. What did Father intend to do with the baby from Sister Philomena's orphanage?

Father Riley, stricken, assumed Keenan had been sent by naval authorities. He admitted they had a baby on board. They were looking for an orphanage in the States.

"What if I told you I wanted to adopt the baby?" Keenan said.

Father Riley gasped. "I'd say God bless you, my son—he's yours!"

They embraced and went looking for Hayward. The captain fired questions at Keenan, but the young surgeon's answers were sensible. The three agreed that George would stay aboard the *Point Cruz*. Since Keenan still had a year to serve, Captain Hayward would try to arrange passage for George to the States.

When the news was announced to the crew at dinner that night, a cheer ripped through the mess.

Back on the *Consolation,* Hugh Keenan was struck by the numbing realization of what he had done. He went at once to the wardroom and wrote his wife. "I am making arrangements to send you a Christmas present that I hope you will love." The days crawled by as he waited for her reply. When it came, the envelope was fat and the letter was long, but the answer was: Yes!

Things were not going well for Father Riley. Korean nationals needed a visa to enter the United States, but when he applied for one, the U.S. consulate told him the quota was filled. Maybe next year.

As time passed, a visa for the baby seemed out of reach. Then, in mid-November, Hayward was invited to a dinner in Seoul where he was to receive a decoration. Vice President Nixon was also scheduled to attend. At the reception there was a good deal of talk about "Chick Hayward's baby"—every flag officer in Korea having heard the story by this time. An admiral friend of Hayward's told Nixon about George and his desperate need for a visa. Nixon turned to Ellis O. Brigg, the American ambassador in Seoul, and spoke the magic words: "Can you help out here?"

Seven days later, the visa came.

In late November, Lieutenant Hugh Keenan kissed his new son good-bye and handed him over to the crew of the *Point Cruz*, which was about to set sail for Japan. Several days later, "1000 uncles" cheered while the bosun's mate piped George Cruz Ascom, IBfc—Infant Boy, first class—over the side, and the baby was turned over to Father Riley, his escort to America via military transport ship.

The *Point Cruz* finally made it back to the United States in December 1953. Father Riley went on to Central America, where he served as a missionary until his death. Chick Hayward, the one-time high school dropout, became a vice admiral and, with the U.S.S. *Enterprise* as his flagship, became the first admiral to command a nuclear task force.

In America, George became Daniel Edward Keenan—Daniel for Hugh's father, Edward for Father Riley. Growing up in Spokane, where his father returned to practice general surgery, Danny dreamed of becoming a sportswriter. He graduated from Washington State University with a degree in communications in 1977. Today he's married and works as sports editor of the biweekly *Grant County Journal* in Ephrata, Washington, a town of 5300.

One by one, the men of the *Point Cruz* had returned to peacetime pursuits, raised families, made careers. Over the years, they lost track of each other, but they never stopped wondering about "their" baby.

Bill Powers, the former hangar-deck chief, had served 30 years in the Navy. He told his four children the story of the baby on the aircraft carrier, told it to his eight grandchildren, and he can hardly wait until his five great-grandchildren are old enough so he can tell it again.

When a reunion of the *Point Cruz* crew was organized for September 1993, Bill was determined to have "George" there. He telephoned Keenan repeatedly, and encouraged him to attend the gathering. "Son, I knew you when you had to be burped after you ate. You have to come!"

Once the word was out that "George" would be there, a special expectancy took hold of the veterans. *Our baby is coming!* The former sailors crowded around to meet a handsome, well-built man, his eyes now turned to brown.

"I would go to the sick bay just to see you," said Donald J. Houlihan, recalling those magic moments in the improvised nursery. "I held you in my arms," one said. "I changed your diapers," another added with a laugh.

On the last night of the reunion, Danny Keenan rose to bid the men farewell. *How do I thank them for saving my life?* he wondered. The faces he looked out upon from the podium where he stood were still strangers to him, but he was touched deeply.

And then the words came. "Without you good men, I wouldn't be here," Danny said quietly. "Not in this hotel, not in this country. And maybe not even on this earth."

Friendship is the only cement that will ever hold the world together.

WOODROW WILSON

194

The men of the *Point Cruz* were ordinary men. They had saved a life without asking for praise or thanks. And now, late in their lives, they could see that their long-ago act of kindness had been something of great importance.

For a moment no one spoke. There was really no need. As it had once been a long time ago on the *Point Cruz,* it was again: Danny Keenan was surrounded by an ocean of fatherly love.

The bird, a nest; the spider, a web; man, friendship.

WILLIAM BLAKE

THE REAL TEST

BY

SUZANNE CHAZIN

I had no notion of what lay in store for me the first time I stepped into David Marain's advanced-math class at Tenafly High School in New Jersey. It was a warm September day in 1977. Someone had opened one of the windows, but I was in a cold sweat. Math terrified me.

At precisely 8:00 A.M., a young rail of a man with black horn-rimmed glasses, a wild floral shirt and dark, receding hair bounded into the room, a black vinyl calculator case strapped on his hip.

"My name's Mr. Ma-*rain*, emphasis on the second syllable," he said brightly. "Not, as I've sometimes been called, Mr. *Mor*-on, emphasis on the first." The class giggled.

I had heard from other students that Mr. Marain was just shy of a Ph.D. in mathematics. It didn't surprise me. He seemed to possess the wit and self-confidence of someone who, without trying, always ran ten steps ahead of the pack. As he bantered with the brightest kids, I sank deeper in despair.

Though Tenafly High brimmed with the precocious children of doctors and lawyers, I was not one of them. At sixteen, I had no special talents, yet inside I was burning with desires and frustrations. Already I had vowed that by age thirty, I would become a novelist, songwriter and world traveler. Math never figured in my future. I was in Mr. Marain's class for another reason.

Advanced math was a prerequisite for calculus and the national Advanced Placement calculus test. Passing the AP exam could earn a student up to a year of college math credits—a big help in keeping down tuition costs. To my parents, this was an incredible bargain. I didn't want to disappoint them.

Mr. Marain scribbled a theorem on the blackboard and asked us to prove it. Carefully, I copied the line of x's, y's and numbers into my notebook. But after a few steps, I was stumped.

Mr. Marain scooted around the room, looking over students' shoulders. I tried to cover the mostly blank sheet of paper with the billowy sleeve of my peasant blouse. Once Mr. Marain realized I wasn't a math whiz, I was certain he'd encourage me to drop out.

Suddenly, from the corner of my eye, I could see him hovering next to me. *This is it,* I told myself. But, instead, he bent down and scratched an equation on the page.

"Try this," he said gently. I did, and from there the theorem seemed to prove itself. "Very good," he said, beaming from behind his glasses, as though I'd arrived at the answer on my own.

I was baffled. This was, after all, an honors class. Why was he taking the trouble to give so much attention to an average student like me?

Later I began to hear stories about how Mr. Marain quietly helped kids deal with all sorts of pressures. He intervened on behalf of students when a grade failed to meet a demanding parent's expectations. If someone couldn't afford a calculator (an expensive item in those days), Mr. Marain loaned his.

He seemed kinder than any teacher I'd ever known, never belittling a student for falling behind in class and never scoffing at a question, no matter how obvious or irrelevant. Most surprising of all, Mr. Marain seemed to make no distinction between the class whiz kids and those who barely scraped by. We were all praised and prodded in equal measure.

Once when the end-of-class bell rang, I walked up to Mr. Marain's desk to ask for help. He smiled expectantly as I approached, but when I opened my book, a shadow of disappointment crossed his face. "I thought you were coming to join the math team," he said.

"Me?" I asked, taken aback. Tenafly High School's math club regularly ranked among the top five in statewide competition. I belonged on it about as much as I belonged on the varsity football squad.

"Why not?" he dared. "You can do it."

I looked at him in disbelief. How could he know the choking fear I felt? Nightly I would struggle with problems, only to discover others had solved them during lunch. But if Mr. Marain could consider me for the math team, perhaps I had a chance after all.

Nevertheless, it was clear I was one of the slowest in class. On our first major exam, I got a C-minus. That afternoon, I went to see Mr. Marain. "I don't belong with the other students," I said, near tears.

I hoped he might find a way to minimize the importance of the grade. Instead, he leaned on his gray metal desk and fixed me in his gaze. "What do you want out of this class?" he asked.

"I don't want to fail," I mumbled.

"You won't fail," he promised. "And I won't let you walk away, as long as you are willing to do your very best." He suggested coming in after school for reviews.

For the first time in my life, I was being asked to probe the limits of my potential. Mr. Marain was demanding excellence from me.

Over the coming months, our after-school reviews took on the regularity of athletic training. "I know math is a struggle for you,"

Mr. Marain said once when I put down the chalk in disgust, unable to solve a problem. "But struggling against obstacles makes us stronger."

I tuned him out. What could he know about struggling and frustration?

My junior year I took a PSAT—sort of a practice Scholastic Aptitude Test—and fared poorly. I was convinced then I'd never be accepted to college or get a decent job.

"Will you feel better if I tell you I had a hard time with tests too?" Mr. Marain asked when I told him the news. "I struggled every inch of the way," he said. "I had to. And so will you."

With Mr. Marain's help, I got a B in advanced math. But I knew that twelfth-grade calculus would be an even greater struggle.

My fears were well-founded. First semester I got a C-plus.

"Hang in there," Mr. Marain said. "A grade doesn't tell the whole story."

It always surprised me that, for a man whose life was numbers, he never accorded them absolute power. Once I got an exam back with a score of 85. On one problem I had the right answer, but Mr. Marain hadn't given me credit.

"You got the answer through luck, not skill," he said when I complained. "But getting lucky works only once, and I don't want you to count on luck in life. I want you to rely on your skills."

My skills were put to the test one Saturday morning in May 1979 when I took the Advanced Placement calculus exam. Weeks later, the results came in. One a scale of one to five, I'd received a four—high enough to get a year of college math credits and save my parents thousands of dollars in tuition.

I thanked Mr. Marain, even wrote a letter to the Board of Education about him. But I knew I would never crack another math book. And if I didn't, what reason would I have to think of him again?

Yet I did think of him. In my twenties, I became a magazine writer. Life seemed full of limitless opportunities. Then I turned thirty, and suddenly I realized I had yet to write the novel or publish the song I had promised myself I would. I couldn't stanch a nagging feeling that I'd stalled somewhere along the way.

It had been a long time since someone had demanded the best of me, and I yearned for that again. So I went back to Tenafly to find Mr. Marain, hoping he could help.

I recognized him instantly as he bounded out of the faculty office. His ring of hair was now gray, his glasses stylishly sleek. Gone were the loud flowered shirts, but otherwise he looked exactly the same.

We talked for a long while, about former times, old friends, struggles and disappointments, mine and—surprisingly—his too.

"I was once in a position similar to the one you're in now," he said.

His father had been a pharmacist who lost his store during the Depression, and the family had been poor. A fat little boy with glasses, he was accepted by other kids only because he could help them with their homework.

The only way he could go to college was on scholarship, so his parents pushed him to excel. He felt overwhelmed at times. "Everyone assumed I was brilliant," he said, "but inside I felt like a fake. I only looked smart because I worked so hard and so much was expected of me."

He graduated as valedictorian of his high-school class and went to Rutgers University on a scholarship to study chemistry. He got a

A true friend never gets in your way unless you happen to be going down.

ARNOLD H. GLASOW

202

summer job as a lab assistant, but he was too clumsy to work with the delicate glassware, and the chemicals made him ill. No matter how hard he struggled, Mr. Marain confided, he realized he would never be a chemist.

Sinking into despair, he dropped out of college the following year, disappointing his parents. He returned later, though, switched to math and set out in the hope of completing a Ph.D.

Later he suffered another setback. His scholarship money began to run out, and he had to accept a teaching job.

In school I never understood why Mr. Marain had such compassion for the underdog. And what could he know about struggling to overcome obstacles, I had asked back then. Now I realized he had been speaking from experience.

But with all his setbacks and disappointments, didn't he feel that he had failed?

"I suppose you might think that," he said. "For a while I had regrets. But is changing direction really failure?" I thought he was now attempting to cushion my own disappointments.

"When you encounter an obstacle in life, what do you do?" he asked, once again the teacher.

"I try to overcome it," I said.

"What if you can't? What if it's like an equation that can't be solved?"

I knew he was developing a chain of reasoning as logical as any math theorem. But where was he headed?

"If you can't overcome it," he said, "you must strike out in a new direction with everything you've got.

"You see," he added, "we all have failures and regrets. The question is what we do with them. No one can always *be* the best," he said. "But if you *do* your best—give everything you've got—you'll either overcome your obstacles or find a new, possibly better direction.

"That's where real success comes from—working hard at something with all your heart and soul."

Then, realizing he was late for a meeting, he rose and embraced me warmly. "Keep reaching for the things you want," he said. "Let time take care of the rest."

A few days later, an envelope arrived. Inside was a poem Mr. Marain had written years ago, called "Ode to a Calculus Class." I remembered him handing it out at the end of senior year. Now I reread the final lines with newfound appreciation:

> But the real test of whether
> > it was worth the pain
> > > will come in a decade or two,
> If a few return and say: "You know,
> > I've learned a lot since then,
> > > but I still remember you."

Here, I thought with a smile, was a David Marain test I would never fail.

The firmest friendships have been formed

in mutual adversity, as iron is most strongly

united by the fiercest flame.

CHARLES CALEB COLTON

WHO MOURNS FOR HERBIE WIRTH?

BY

JOSEPH P. BLANK

When the minister left his church that cold winter morning, he expected to see no more than a half-dozen or so mourners at the grave of Herbert A. Wirth. It was a below-freezing, windy, bleak day, and snow was beginning to fall. The services over the body would be brief, probably almost perfunctory.

Two days earlier, a mortuary executive had telephoned the minister, explaining that Wirth had no family and that his body was unclaimed, and asking him to perform the burial rites. The minister never refused such requests, even when, as in this case, he could say virtually nothing in a eulogy. Wirth hadn't been a member of his church, or indeed of any church.

The minister knew only that the old man had peddled household sundries from door to door in Indianapolis's Northside area. The minister's wife had bought dishcloths from him, and he vaguely remembered having seen Wirth: "A small man, his gray hair always carefully combed, never pushy, always polite. He never had anything in particular we wanted to buy, but we always bought." Who would come to the funeral of such a man?

Herbert Wirth didn't feel he was really important to anyone in this world. He was seventy-three years old, slightly more than five feet tall, a little bird of a man who looked as if he weighed no more than 100 pounds. He had no family; no friends exchanged visits with him; he lived alone in a neat, white, frame house left to him by his mother, who died in 1957.

Off and on for 27 years, and at least six days a week for the last 11 years of his life, Herbie—very few people knew his last name—was on the streets. He carried two large paper shopping bags filled with washcloths, dishcloths, pot holders, pot scrapers, red and blue bandannas, and shoelaces. Each item cost 25 cents, except for fancy, handwoven pot holders made by a teenage girl on his street. He sold these for her at 50 cents apiece, and refused to take a commission. "I can't buy these pretty pot holders from my supplier," he told her. "And it's a service to my customers for me to have them."

Each morning he left his house at about 8:30 and set off on a carefully planned route that would bring him home in eight or nine hours. He didn't think of himself as a peddler. "I'm a salesman," he'd explain to old customers, "and I use psychology in my work. I carry only the best quality goods. I work out my routes so that I visit each house exactly three times a year. That way I don't make a nuisance of myself. I'm polite. Whether or not you buy from me, my 'thank you' is the same. I want people to think of me as a nice person."

After offering, "Pot holders today? A nice red bandanna for your little boy?" in a high-pitched voice, Herbie always hoped to linger and chat for a while. It was the way he eased his loneliness. He reminisced about his mother, to whom he had been very close. Every Sunday during the warm months, he visited Crown Hill Cemetery and adorned her grave with a bouquet. He owned the adjacent plot, and the double headstone contained room for his name and dates. In March 1968, he had picked out a gray casket for himself and prepaid his funeral expenses, which came to $749.26.

Herbie nurtured a regret that most of his customers heard several times: "I should have gotten married when I was young. It's a lonely life without a family. I have nobody." He made his statement as a fact, not as a request for pity.

And the housewife, uneasy, eager to get back to her chores, yet touched by the poignancy of Herbie's reflection, would say, "That's not so, Herbie! You have lots of friends."

"Well, I do run into a lot of people in my work," he'd reply. Then he'd pick up his shopping bags and, with little, quick steps that were half shuffle, half jog, hurry on to the next house. Whether it was summer, and the heat made his brow glisten with perspiration, or winter, when the cold made his slightly bulging eyes water and his nose run, the thin, stooped figure never altered its pace.

While it was never his intention, Herbie sometimes was a nuisance. More than one too-busy housewife had seen him trotting up the walk and decided not to answer his knock. But most women who did so felt guilty, and usually compensated by over-buying on his next visit.

Everybody liked his pride, self-respect and independence. He earned his living the hard way, asking for nothing—except perhaps a glass of water on a hot day. And he never peddled his wares to the houses close to his own. "I'm your neighbor," he explained to the women who offered to buy from him. "And I want you to know me as a neighbor, not as a salesman at your door."

He raked leaves and shoveled snow for some of his customers, and in this tiring work, too, he did his best. "I may be a little slow, but I do a good job," he said proudly.

Late each afternoon, his rounds completed, Herbie stopped at the service station a block and a half from his home. Here he converted his two pocketfuls of change into bills, and sat around the office for a while, chewing the fat and frequently eating a quart of vanilla ice cream. "I don't smoke or drink," he often announced. "But vanilla ice cream—that's my vice."

At home, he made his dinner—usually canned salmon, canned vegetables, and bread thickly coated with peanut butter. Then he meticulously cleaned the house, did his laundry and shined his shoes while listening to classical music on the radio.

Every Saturday morning, he walked 18 blocks to a supermarket that carried his favorite bread. He arrived a few minutes before it was stacked on the shelves. After he had bought his week's supply and taken it home, he resumed work.

On January 30, a Saturday, Herbie shoveled snow off a few driveways, then appeared at the supermarket at his usual time. While waiting for the bread delivery, he wordlessly collapsed and died.

That day, a few of Herbie's neighbors learned of his death. Most of them took a long pause in whatever they were doing when they heard the news. Herbie's biggest complaint had been an occasional headache, and no one had ever known him to be sick. It was hard to believe that the wizened, scurrying little man, his shoulders growing more stooped with the years, would never again be seen on the streets.

Two days later, Herbie's name appeared in the newspaper notices of scheduled funerals. Several of his customers called one another to ask, "Is that our Herbie?"

The wife of an attorney telephoned a mortuary and asked, "How do you handle the funeral of a person who has no family or friends?"

"Well, we get a minister to say prayers," was the reply. "Two or three of us accompany the casket to the cemetery and attend the services. We just do the best we can."

How terrible that Herbie won't have anyone he knows at his funeral! the woman thought. *Well, he will. I'll be there.* The same thought was crystallizing in the minds of other people who had known Herbie. A widow told her next-door neighbor, "An awful thing has happened! Herbie died."

The neighbor said, "I was thinking about him yesterday. I've been waiting to buy dishcloths from him." She began to cry.

"He has nobody," her friend said. "Nobody. You and I have to go."

"Yes, we must be there."

On the day before the funeral, a reporter for the Indianapolis *Star*, who had once interviewed Herbie Wirth about his life as a peddler, wrote an obituary in which he mentioned that Herbie had told him of a fear that no one would attend his funeral. For most of Herbie's Northside customers, this was the first news of his death.

That night, adults and teenagers all around the neighborhood talked and thought about Herbie. His loneliness connected, suddenly, with the loneliness they had felt at one time or another. They were moved by his anxiety that no one would bid him a last good-bye, and many resolved to attend the funeral, even if it meant being there alone.

A leading automobile dealer who, a short time previously, had suffered a heart attack remembered the time his car got stuck in the snow on his driveway. Doctor's orders forbade him to shovel. Suddenly, Herbie appeared and cleared away the snow. The dealer told his wife, "I'm going to Herbie's funeral." She nodded and said, "I am, too."

For some people, Herbie's funeral was a private, personal obligation. It wasn't talked about. Hundreds left for work at the normal hour—and were surprised to meet their wives at the cemetery. High-school and

A true friend is the greatest of all blessings, and that which we take the least care of all to acquire.

LA ROCHEFOUCAULD

college students cut classes—and unexpectedly found themselves nodding greetings to their parents.

Old and young, rich and poor, black and white, they began converging on the cemetery at nine o'clock, an hour before the scheduled services. Mink coats mingled with bell-bottom trousers and worn cloth coats. Servicemen in uniform and businessmen in dark suits strode across the sprawling 540-acre Crown Hill Cemetery toward the grave. Old people, some with canes, wearily but determinedly trudged along. Truck drivers, cabbies and delivery men parked outside the cemetery and walked nearly a mile to the grave site. Young mothers carried small children, trying to shield them from the icy wind.

The minister was stopped two blocks from the cemetery by streets jammed with vehicles. He circled toward another entrance. Inside the cemetery, employees were directing the traffic that was choking the narrow roadways. The puzzled minister tried to recall what well-known figure was being buried that day. He parked; and then, as he walked toward the grave, he realized suddenly that all these people must be coming to attend the funeral of Herbert Wirth. It stunned him.

The cemetery wasn't prepared for the crowd. "Our entire staff was out, trying to control the situation, but it couldn't," the director said later. "There must have been six hundred cars. Nobody knows how many more were parked farther away, or how many cars couldn't get near the cemetery and left."

Robert C. Braun, executive director of the Historic Landmarks Foundation of Indiana, had also remembered Herbie and his shopping bags, and decided to attend the funeral in case nobody else did. Now, like others, he was astonished at the hundreds of people moving toward the grave. Then he recalled that the old 1888 cemetery bell, hanging five stories high in the tower above the cemetery's historic waiting station, had just been re-roped. The bell had probably not been rung in more than 40 years. Walking to the bell rope, he began pulling on it, sending out clear, measured rings that could be heard for two miles. He tolled for a half hour, wearing blisters on his hands. Then he sounded the death knell: single rings separated by long, mournful pauses.

At 10:30, as the snow fell, the minister gazed around him at a crowd of more than 1000. He caught "a glow from those people; they *wanted* to be with Herbie Wirth." He began a brief, deeply felt eulogy in which he said, "Herbert Wirth never dreamed he had so many friends. In this cold and sometimes uncaring world, surely God must be pleased today."

When the prayers were completed, the crowd lingered on. A sense of camaraderie was tying strangers together. Some people were exhilarated. Some experienced a deep satisfaction. Everybody felt good about being there, and nobody was in a hurry to leave the scene that made them feel good.

"Herbie created a mood that day," a businessman reflected later. "He gave me a new respect for human beings."

Herbie Wirth had always paid his own way in life. He asked only that a few people appear at his funeral. What he gave for this favor far exceeded what he asked for.

We take care of our health, we lay up
money, we make our roof tight and our
clothing sufficient, but who provides wisely
that he shall not be wanting in the best
property of all—friends?

RALPH WALDO EMERSON

CABIN ON THE HILL

BY

HENRY HURT

Good memories are the most precious of our treasures. Nurtured and caressed, they remain with us all our lives, like favorite books to be plucked from a shelf and enjoyed. But sometimes an otherwise marvelous memory is blemished in a way that brings guilt and uncertainty. This happened to me. The experience goes back 35 years to my childhood in rural Virginia . . .

In those soft days so long ago, my closest friends were Lou Coles and her ten children. They lived in a log cabin within hollering distance of our house. I especially liked Louis Coles and two of his brothers. Every day we would holler back and forth, urgently discussing our plans.

Lou Coles, a magnificent matriarch whose husband had long departed, was a stout woman who usually kept her head wrapped in a kerchief. The Coles cabin had two small rooms downstairs and one upstairs. The logs were hewn pine with mud daubing to keep out the cold. A wood stove was used for cooking and heat. The cabin sat on a hill among large shade trees, surrounded by acres of cow pasture. Sometimes the whole herd of cows, along with a few pigs, would be standing in the yard. There was no road to the cabin, or any reason for one. The Coleses did their traveling by foot.

I suppose I loved the Coleses as dearly as I did my own little sister. To me, their lives seemed idyllic, even though the bigger children spent long days laboring in the tobacco fields. Their water came from a hand-dug well and their light from kerosene lamps. But there was a warmth about their lives that I longed to share—and did.

The cabin had an aroma to it that I suspect has vanished from the earth forever. Even in summer, the stove was going most of the day, with old Lou boiling and simmering and frying food for the table. The beans and greens would cook slowly for hours, filling the hollow with the scent of wood smoke and pork fat, sometimes seasoned with a pungent odor of turnips or the fragrance of hot biscuits and hoecakes.

It was my good fortune to have an extraordinary mother who allowed me to spend plenty of time with the Coleses—though, in reality, she couldn't have kept us apart. (When she tried, we simply hollered back and forth all day.) She gave the Coles boys strict orders to make me take turns, share everything and act nice. In this respect, our lives seemed equal and hardly ever separate.

My special friend was Louis, for he was closest to my age. The palms of his black hands were light, and I remember—that summer in the South in 1948—telling him the old Uncle Remus fable: Once upon a time *all* humanity was black. Word spread that there was a special pond in which the black could be washed off. But by the time the laziest people reached the pond, there was only enough water to wash off the palms of their hands and the soles of their feet. "And that," I explained to Louis as we waded in the creek in the hollow, chasing crawfish, "is why I'm white all over and you're not."

And Louis cheerfully agreed. Then we splashed through the creek until old Lou hollered for us to come up to the house and dry our clothes. We would fly. She was good with a switch, but completely amiable as long as everyone in sight was behaving properly.

Along with their good manners, the Coles boys were high-spirited and imaginative. They could have fun with anything. When my little red wagon wouldn't roll down the rutted hill, Louis produced a huge, worn-out tractor tire. He and I would curl up together inside it and go careering down the hill, smashing into stumps and rocks until we hit the creek bed.

But even country boys occasionally had to go to town. There was a moving-picture house in Chatham, a mile away. The Coles boys and I would scavenge along the road for soda bottles, which we redeemed for two cents each at Ham Williams's store. Six bottles were worth a movie ticket.

The movies were sensational—especially the cowboys and the weekly serials. But it was lonesome sitting downstairs by myself when I could hear my friends whooping in ecstasy above me. The balcony was reserved for "Colored," and my attempts to get into that section were politely discouraged by the manager.

The crowning moment of those Saturday afternoons was after the movie. We'd all meet out front and start for home. Then the tales would begin. I would make up outlandish events I had seen in *my* movie, while the Coles boys would make up events they had seen in *theirs*. Until the next Saturday, Louis and I would argue joyously about who had seen the better movie.

At that age, the fact that our great friendship had to stop at the door to the movies was only an irritant to our boisterous fun. Later, it came to bother me deeply. And so did what happened at Christmastime.

I was hardly more than a toddler the first Christmas morning I left my bounty of gifts in our warm brick house and ran over to see what

Santa had left at the Coles cabin. To my shock, Santa had left . . . *nothing*. How could Santa be so generous at my house and not even stop at the cabin across the hollow? This was a question even my wise parents could not answer.

The only gift I remember the Coles family receiving was the brightly wrapped box Mother would fix for them on Christmas Eve. It was filled with fruit, nuts, candy, a sack of flour or coffee, and a useful little gift for old Lou and each child. The present I best recall was a flannel nightgown for one of the girls, decorated with little animal figures. That Christmas night, in the dark little cabin, old Lou and the children sat, staring quietly, a little fearfully, at the nightie. We had failed to tell them that the figures glowed in the dark.

Meanwhile, I lay in a warm bed in a room all my own, thinking of my pile of presents and trying to figure out why Santa stayed away from the cabin on the hill.

Around 1952, when I was ten, the Coles family moved to a big tobacco farm. Except for a few brief encounters in town, they vanished from my life. Then we heard that they had moved again, this time too far even for them to walk to Chatham.

Everything became busy for me. I went off to boarding school and then to college. In my mind, old Lou and the children were with me every step of the way, providing my best memories— but memories becoming increasingly bittersweet. My heart panged especially at Christmastime. When I was home, I would ask about the Coleses. People said that a couple of children were still somewhere in the county, but most of them had gone north. Then I heard that old Lou had died. To me, that was the end of the Coles family—except in my memories.

In the mid-1960s, I wound up in Mississippi as a newspaper reporter covering civil rights. I remember one hot day standing in a roiling, angry crowd in Philadelphia, Mississippi, a few miles from where three civil-rights workers had been killed. The crowd was there to hear Martin Luther King. I did not believe that I or my people were all as bad as King insisted, but his eloquence caused some inward churning of my memories of Louis and his brothers. While I had loved and enjoyed the Coleses, had I simply used these black people for my fun and entertainment? I wasn't sure. But it did seem that all I gave them in return was a trifling Christmas box, as if to say, "You're not good enough for Santa Claus, but this box should make you happy."

After leaving Mississippi, I married and settled in New York. Many times I told my wife about Louis and his brothers—about my cherished memories of my childhood with them. I spoke of how guilty I felt about the Coleses, their lives, their cabin, especially my memories of the Christmas box and the absence of Santa Claus. What made me feel worse, of course, were my happy memories of how much I *enjoyed* them, and how much I loved their cabin and the way they lived.

On visits to Virginia, I continued to inquire about the Coleses, particularly Louis, my special friend. But down deep, I suppose that I really didn't want to find them. I was certain their memories would be starkly different from my own.

Margaret and I soon had three children, and each Christmas I felt a tightening in my throat and a heaviness in my heart as I looked at the piles of presents under our tree and the bounty from Santa in front of the blazing fireplace. "Daddy," a child would say, "you look so sad. What's wrong?"

Hold a true friend with both your hands.

NIGERIAN PROVERB

218

"Nothing," I'd answer. "Just something about the Coles family. I'll explain it someday." Margaret would squeeze my hand, for she alone understood.

Then, nearly 20 years after I had left home, we bought the old house in Chatham where my parents had lived when I was born. Nothing has ever thrilled me more than getting my family back home. We happened to arrive on my thirty-seventh birthday. That night, in my happiness, I slept outside with my head on the Virginia soil. But even then, as I lay there considering my extraordinary blessings, I thought about old Lou and her children. They had become to me a symbol of black families scattered and lost across America, their rich personalities and bright intelligence forever blurred and subdued.

My mother still lives a couple of miles away in the house where I grew up. And across the road, just within hollering distance, sits the cabin on the hill. My mother owns it now, and we keep hay there for our horses. Often when I am stacking bales, I stop for a moment to feel the fun and laughter I knew in those tiny rooms. How could I have loved it all so much—and now be so deeply troubled by it?

Then one Saturday in September, I was at my desk when the telephone rang. "My name is Louis Coles," a voice said. "I don't know if you remember me, but . . ."

"Louis!" I hollered, my eyes brimming with tears. "How can you ask if I *remember* you? I've been thinking about you for thirty years!"

Louis returned my exuberance in kind, explaining that I had been a constant fixture in his memory, that he had often wanted to seek me out. We repeated the same things, asked the same questions, and laughed and laughed as our memories mingled. I learned that for the past 21 years Louis has worked at Glassboro State College in New Jersey, where he is now in a supervisory position. Louis's wife, Brenda, has worked for

Mobil Oil for the past ten years. They have two children, and own a house on a gentle hill in the country.

Louis reported that his brothers and sisters are doing well, too. They are happily settled in different spots from Virginia to New York—all working and most with families.

A few weeks later, Louis and I got together in Chatham. More than six feet tall, Louis is an affable man, with the same energetic spontane-

ity he had as a child. It was too chilly for us to go splash through a creek, but we did catch and skin a mess of catfish and try to fry them the way old Lou used to. We failed to measure up to her standards, but this did not mar our delight in making the effort.

We also drove out to those few acres of earth that frame our childhood memories. We leaned against the fence and gazed over at the little cabin on the hill. Neither of us was able to say much. "Let's walk over there," Louis finally said. "I'd like to just touch it and smell it. You know, that cabin gave me everything I ever needed. Love and warmth. Plenty to eat." As we ambled toward the cabin, around a small pond that now fills the hollow, Louis added, "One of the biggest things we had were you and your family. You were our best friends. Especially you, Henry, because you always gave us so much entertainment." He chuckled fondly.

"That's funny," I said. "I always thought *you* provided *me* with entertainment."

"Then we must have been having a lot of fun!" said Louis.

We became solemn as we opened the cabin door. Louis gently, lovingly, inspected every corner, remembering precisely where everything had been. And then we began to talk quietly of serious things—racism, black poverty and the old segregationist South. It was clear that we both understood how profoundly wrong the old way was, and that the passing of that way made it possible for the Coles children to reach beyond the balcony of the Chatham movie house and the tobacco fields of Virginia. Yet, Louis insisted that as a child he never felt the bite of racism. I mentioned how we used to go to the motion-picture house and be separated at the door. Didn't *that* bother him? "Why would it, Henry?" I could sense a hidden grin. "The movies *I* saw were always better than the ones you saw!" Our roaring laughter quickly took us back 35 years.

But I was still puzzled about how the little cabin could be so important to Louis. What had he found here that could fuel his life with happiness and success?

"The most important thing came from my momma," he said. "She taught all of us that folks are going to treat you just like you treat them. And that's all I've ever done. When you understand that, it makes it real easy to get along in life." He brushed a tear from his eye.

"Let me ask you about something that still bothers me," I said. "At Christmas, Santa always came to our house, but he never stopped at this cabin. I can see you right now, Louis, standing in our living room staring down at those piles of presents." I had to bite my lip. "And I knew you'd be lucky to get *one* present."

"Come on, Henry," said Louis, brightening. "I *loved* for you to get all those new toys. Because then you gave me all your *old* toys!"

Louis's rich laughter washed over me, filling the little cabin and cleansing my memories forever. What greater gift can one man give another?

FROM STREET KIDS TO ROYAL KNIGHTS

BY

JO COUDERT

A whoosh of flame startled teacher Bill Hall as he walked into his classroom. Whirling around, he saw fifteen-year-old José Tavarez holding a lighter to a spray can of deodorant. "Make *bueno* blowtorch," the Puerto Rican teenager was explaining to a classmate. Confiscating the can, Hall also broke up an arm-wrestling bout between a Pakistani and an Ecuadorean boy and gestured to Sze Wai Chen, newly arrived from Hong Kong, to put away his Chinese newspaper.

Sze Wai, age thirteen, pointed to the chess set Hall carried: "How say English?"

"Do you play?" Hall asked. Sze Wai shook his head no. Hall wondered if the student had understood the question.

Recently transferred to J.H.S. 99 in New York City's East Harlem, Hall taught English as a second language, but he was not having much success with these kids. They were all troublemakers, some guilty of chronic truancy, vandalism or thievery. Most had an attention span measurable only in milliseconds.

Sze Wai's interest in the chess set was the first flicker of curiosity from any of them. Hoping to reach these kids any way he could, Hall, a veteran teacher of 24 years, opened the board and set out the pieces. "Chess is a war game," he began, "a fight between two people, like boxing or wrestling." As he held up each chess piece, he wrote the English name on the blackboard. The class quieted. "If any of you guys want to learn how to play," Hall said, "come around after school today."

At three o'clock, when prime mischief-makers Tony Pagán and José Tavarez slouched in, Hall felt a wave of apprehension. *Together these guys could take me,* he thought. But the teenagers never looked up from the chessboard as Hall described the strategic importance of controlling the board's center. At the end of the session, Pagán mumbled, "Heavy, man."

"Cool," echoed Tavarez. "Now we chess players."

"No," Hall corrected him. "Now you know how the pieces move."

To Hall's surprise, the two boys were back the next afternoon, along with José Luis Ortiz and Javier Montaño. Tavarez paired off against Pagán and immediately moved to control the center. *The school must have been mistaken in labeling him an underachiever,* Hall thought. Soon, Sze Wai Chen and two Pakistani brothers, Bashart and Zia Choudhry, joined in. As the group grew, Hall began giving up his lunch hours and Saturday mornings to teach the basics of the game and supervise play.

Fellow teachers told him he was a sucker. "You're wasting your time," said one. "These kids haven't got the brains to come in out of the rain."

"Why not play a game with them?" challenged Hall. When the teacher showed up, Pagán creamed him. "Maybe the problem with teaching these kids is our low expectations for them," Hall said.

The day Pagán checkmated Hall himself, the teacher sat back and whistled. "Hey, you guys are getting good!" Pagán grinned with pride.

"You teach us more?" one of the boys asked anxiously. "You teach us traps and sacrifices?"

"If you want to learn," Hall said, "you'll have to read chess books."

"In English?" one groaned.

"If what we need to know is in English, we'll read English," Pagán announced firmly.

The boys' comprehension and vocabulary soon began to improve. When a science teacher remarked on Tavarez's heightened concentration, the teenager explained the change: "I used to give up if I didn't understand. But I don't do that anymore, because if you give up on the chessboard, you're dead."

One Saturday night Hall crammed his Volkswagen with kids and took them downtown to a chess club. "Get those street punks out of here," an old-timer growled. Montaño stepped forward. "Sir," he said, "we'd appreciate it if you'd play with us. We need the competition."

Grudgingly, the old-timer took him on. When Montaño made a move that exposed his queen, the old-timer waved forgivingly. "You don't want to do that, boy. Take it back." Montaño shook his head. "Mr. Hall says if we make mistakes, we have to take the consequences." With his queen duly captured, the boy made two more moves and checkmated his opponent. "You fell for a trap that's two hundred years old," Montaño said gravely. "You'll find it in a book called *The Art of Checkmate.*"

Hall considered entering the boys in the 1986 New York City Interscholastic Chess League Spring Tournament, even though they'd been playing only four months. "Don't," advised Edward Rodriguez, principal of J.H.S. 99. "They'll get whipped by one of the private schools, and the self-esteem and self-confidence chess has given them will be destroyed."

But the boys were not worried. "Who says we're gonna lose, man?" Ortiz demanded. "We're goin'."

How can I take such a ragged-looking bunch to a tournament? thought Hall. They need uniforms—and a team name. Since chess is known as the royal game and knights represent the gentlemen warriors, Hall ordered a dozen red T-shirts emblazoned "ROYAL KNIGHTS—J.H.S. 99."

He wondered if the boys might refuse to wear anything so square. He need not have worried. Moreover, within a few days, he noticed that their tough-guy street mannerisms were disappearing. They asked Hall to show them the proper way to shake hands. "We're gonna win," they said. "But in case we don't, we gotta know how to lose like gentlemen."

Ortiz won first place in the individual competition, Montaño second place among seventh-graders. Even the boys who had been defeated were exultant. They were the Royal Knights now, and a win for one was a win for all.

By now the New York papers, delighted to have a story out of East Harlem that wasn't about drugs or violence, had made the boys local celebrities. And Faneuil Adams, a retired Mobil Oil executive, offered to finance the team's trip to Syracuse, New York, to play in the 1986 state tournament. But the boys refused to go.

Hall was stunned, until he realized the Knights were frightened—not of competing, but of not knowing how to handle themselves in hotels, trains and restaurants.

"Okay," he said, "forget Syracuse. But let's celebrate this win. I'm taking the team to dinner."

At the restaurant, Hall began musing aloud over the menu. "I see we get a choice of a first course: soup or fruit cup. I don't want to eat too much because then comes the main course, over on this side of the menu . . ."

The boys, busy watching which fork Hall used and how he cut his meat, left most of the conversation to their teacher, who spoke of places he'd been, trains he'd taken, and hotels he'd stayed at. A few days later Pagán announced the team had decided it might be possible to go to the tournament after all.

At the station they turned up carrying their belongings in shopping bags and cardboard suitcases tied with rope. One boy's jeans were out at the knees, another's sneakers were ripped and flopping. Hall took them across the street to a clothing store and bought them replacements.

On the train, the Knights set up their chess sets and began practicing. Soon they had an audience. "East Harlem, eh?" one man whispered to another. "I wonder how many are into drugs."

Pagán overheard him. "None of us," he said. "We're into chess."

At the tournament, Alexis Ortega had already clinched third place when Eduardo Santana began playing for fourth. It was a tense game. Suddenly Santana made a crazy move. Hall stiffened, but Tavarez gave him an almost imperceptible wink that said, "It's a street move, man. Keep cool."

Santana's opponent hesitated, reached for a piece, pulled back. Finally he took the gambit, and Santana moved crisply, in a beautifully played end game and checkmate.

A few weeks later Hall was called to the principal's office. *Which team member is in trouble?* he wondered. The Knights had come to be known as his boys, and he was called in whenever there was a problem.

Entering the principal's office, Hall found the Knights lined up in front of Rodriguez. "Good Lord!" he exclaimed. "Is the whole team in trouble?" Eduardo Santana stepped forward, started bravely on the speech he'd memorized, and choked up as a plaque was handed to Hall. "For Mr. Hall," it read. "We hope that this plaque helps to show how

Don't make friends who are comfortable to be with. Make friends who will force you to lever yourself up.

THOMAS J. WATSON, SR.

much we appreciate what you have done for us. Many thanks from all of us. The Royal Knights of East Harlem."

A year and a half after they first started playing, the Knights flew to California to compete in the 1987 National Junior High School Chess Tournament. Faneuil Adams again helped with the expenses. Not only did the Royal Knights come in seventeenth out of 109 teams from 35 states, but by now they were beginning to act like seasoned travelers.

Two of the Knights, José Laó and Sze Wai Chen, were later invited to the Manhattan Chess Club to play an exhibition against Maya Chiburdanidze, the women's world chess champion from the Soviet Union. The two were among those holding out longest against Chiburdanidze's championship play, and afterward Hall spotted the three of them talking together.

"Maya says we should go to the Soviet Union and play the kids there," reported Sze Wai. Hall was speechless. The Knights would be the first American scholastic chess team ever to visit the Soviet Union. But Hall could already hear the chorus of people saying, "You're crazy. Can't be done. Too expensive." *In addition,* he thought, *the school administration will probably veto the idea.*

He was wrong. So Hall continued rounding up corporate and private donations, and made the arrangements with Soviet chess officials. New York banking executive Bob Moore and his wife, Mimi, bought luggage for the boys, and an exclusive men's clothing store outfitted the team.

Meanwhile, the Knights urged Hall to impose an almost military discipline. When one boy didn't show up for a practice session, he was dropped from the team. "Actions have consequences," Hall reminded him. "You've learned that in chess, and it's true in life too." The boy was reinstated, but only after he got permission from each teammate to return.

When the team arrived in Moscow, members of the Soviet Sports Committee met the boys and escorted them to their hotel for a festive dinner. The next day, at the Central Chess Club, the team was surprised at the youthfulness of their opponents, who were only ten and eleven years old—and shocked when every Knight was quickly routed.

Back at the hotel, they sat in gloomy silence. "Look," Hall told them, "they start these kids when they're five years old. Of course they're good. But now you know their style, and tomorrow they'll be overconfident. You'll do better."

The next morning, in a demonstration match against international grandmaster E. Sveshnikov, Pagán finished in a draw. This lifted the team's spirits, and that afternoon, playing against Soviet youths, the Knights achieved a 50–50 split.

Later at one of Moscow's newer youth centers, the team was warned that the competition would be the stiffest yet. Even so, Hall was surprised when Tavarez emerged after only 15 minutes in the tournament room. "That sure was a quick loss," said Hall.

"Who lost?" asked Tavarez, beaming. "I won!" That night Bashart Choudhry got a draw against a young Soviet champion, and the whole team celebrated. They had demonstrated to the Soviets, among the strongest scholastic chess players in the world, that the street-smart kids from East Harlem could control the center.

"It isn't that winning's so important," Tavarez explained to Hall. "It's proving you *can* win. I don't want to leave the board until I prove that the guy who beat me isn't indestructible."

How they've changed, Hall thought as he walked down the aisle of the plane on the trip home. They had grown into thoughtful young men willing to take responsibility and able to plan ahead. That morning, one of the boys had teased Bashart Choudhry about his intention of becoming a lawyer. "Life is no different than chess," Choudhry had said. "If you don't have a plan, you'll get beaten."

Hall dropped into the empty seat beside Pagán, who was writing in the journal he'd kept on the trip. "Maybe someday you'll write a novel about kids growing up in East Harlem," remarked Hall.

"Yeah. Remember what a pain I was?"

"Now you're talking about going to college," Hall marveled. "It's great what chess has done for you."

"Chess *has* been good for us," Pagán agreed. "But if I write that book, it won't be dedicated to chess. It'll be dedicated to the teacher who taught us the importance of controlling the center—and that the center is really ourselves."

THE THIRTEENTH MISSION

BY
FLIGHT LIEUTENANT
GEORGE PATRICK BROPHY,
as told to David MacDonald

According to official records of the Royal Canadian Air Force, I owe my life to "a miraculous escape." But was it only an amazing twist of fate that saved me from certain death? Or was there something more—another man's incredible courage—that helped me live to tell the tale? Even now, I still wonder.

That June night in 1944, at 419 Squadron's base in England, our seven-man crew was sitting on the grass by our Lancaster bomber, waiting to take off for France. For us, it was a night of mixed omens. A few hours earlier we'd been briefed for a raid on the railway yards at Cambrai—our crew's thirteenth mission. Moreover, we were due on target shortly after midnight, June 13.

Then, as if to compensate, a turret gunner named Andy Mynarski, my closest buddy in the crew, found a four-leaf clover in the grass. Twirling the good-luck token like a tiny propeller, he turned to me. "Here, Pat," he said. "*You* take it."

230

Minutes later our black, four-engine "Lanc"—*A for Able*—was climbing into the darkness, one of 200 bombers that RCAF 6 Group sent out that night, a week after D-Day, to pound German supply lines. I sat alone in the Lanc's glass-domed rear turret, watching the evening stars pop out. As the "Tail-End Charlie," I was shut off behind the revolving turret's doors, far from all my crewmates. My only contact with them was via the intercom, on which pilot Art deBreyne's voice now crackled briefly: "Estimating eighty minutes more to target."

"Thanks," came Andy Mynarski's reply from the mid-upper turret. "No rush."

In our crew, which had been together for a year, Andy was a relative newcomer. Four months earlier, before our first mission, he'd turned up to replace a gunner who'd gone to the hospital.

At twenty-seven, Andy was a quiet, chunky fellow with a slow, boyish grin. The son of Polish immigrants, he had grown up in Winnipeg and left school at sixteen, when his father died, to help support four kid brothers and sisters. After joining the army in 1941, he'd switched to the RCAF because most of his friends were in it. To Andy, friends were important.

We soon became close chums. Since I was an officer and Andy an NCO, rank kept us in different quarters. But we made light of it. Splitting up on the base after a mission or a pub-crawl in town, I'd clap him on the back and say, "So long, Irish." He'd stiffen, exaggerate a salute and reply with a hint of Polish accent, "Good night, *sir.*"

In a tight spot, I could always count on him. Once, on leave in London with Andy and two other crewmates, I got into a late-night scrap and phoned them from a police station. They laughed and said a taste of jail would teach me a lesson. While the others went back to sleep, however, Andy got up to bail me out.

But one thing Andy would not do. Even on practice flights, he would not go into the tail turret. Like most air gunners, he hated its cramped isolation. "Back there," he said, "you're completely cut off."

Back there now, as we crossed the French coast, I saw enemy searchlights sweeping the sky, then lazy puffs of smoke and deceptively pretty sunbursts of sparks. "Light flak below, skipper," I reported.

Suddenly, with a blinding flash, a searchlight caught us. Others quickly converged. "Hang on!" called deBreyne. "We're coned!" He threw the Lanc into a banking dive, then swung upward, trying to squirm away from the deadly glare. Then, just as suddenly, we were in the dark again.

We'd escaped—or had we? The Germans sometimes *let* a bomber shake loose, once their night fighters got a fix on it. It was too soon to tell.

Past the coastal defenses, we began a slow descent. This was to be a low-level raid, from 2000 feet. We were down to 5000 feet when I caught a fleeting glimpse of a twin-engine fighter. "Bogey astern!" I yelled on the intercom. "Six o'clock!" Instantly, as he'd done to evade the searchlights, deBreyne began to corkscrew. Seconds later I saw a JU-88 streaking up from below. "He's coming under us!"

As I whirled my turret around and opened fire, the white-bellied Junkers flashed by with its cannons blazing. Three sharp explosions rocked our aircraft. Two shots knocked out both port engines and set a wing tank on fire. The third tore into the fuselage, starting another fire between Andy's turret and mine.

We began losing altitude fast. I listened for orders on the intercom, but it was dead. Then a red light flashed in my turret—the signal to bail out. *A for Able* was doomed. For some reason, I glanced at my watch. It was 13 minutes past midnight, June 13.

While Art deBreyne fought to keep the plane from heeling over in a spiral dive, bomb-aimer Jack Friday tugged at the forward crew's escape hatch. It flew open with the violent updraft, hit his head and knocked him out. Jack was still unconscious when flight engineer Roy Vigars dropped him through the hole, yanked his D-string and jumped after him. Navigator Bob Bodie went next, then wireless operator Jim Kelly. When pilot Art deBreyne finally jumped—from barely 800 feet—he felt sure that Andy Mynarski and I had both already succeeded in getting out of the rear hatch.

But he was wrong.

To fire, I'd swung my turret to port. Now I had to straighten it out so I could go back into the plane for my parachute and then jump from the rear door. I pressed the rotation pedal. Nothing happened. The hydraulic system had been shattered, locking my turret at such an angle that I couldn't get out. Meanwhile, inside the fuselage, flames were sweeping toward me.

Don't panic, I told myself. *There's still another way.* I managed to open the turret doors a few inches, reached in for my parachute and clipped it on. Then I began hand-cranking the turret to the beam position, where I'd be able to flip right out into the slipstream. To my horror, the rotating gear broke off. Now there was *no* way out. At that moment, imprisoned in a falling plane, I remembered Andy Mynarski's words: "Back there, you're completely cut off."

Then I saw him. Andy had slid down from the mid-upper turret and made his way back to the rear escape hatch, about 15 feet from me. Just as he was about to jump, he glanced around and spotted me through the Plexiglas part of my turret. One look told him I was trapped.

Instantly, he turned away from the hatch—his doorway to safety—and started toward me. With the aircraft lurching drunkenly, Andy couldn't keep his feet. He got down on hands and knees and crawled—straight through blazing hydraulic oil. By the time he reached the tail, his

When you learn to live for others, they will live for you.

PARAMAHANSA YOGANANDA

233

flying suit was on fire. I shook my head—it was hopeless. "Don't try!" I shouted. I waved him away.

Andy didn't seem to notice. Completely ignoring his own plight, he grabbed a fire axe and tried to smash the turret free. It gave slightly, but not enough. Wild with desperation, he tore at the doors with his bare hands—in vain. By now he was a mass of flames below the waist. Seeing him like that, I forgot everything else. Over the roar of wind and the whine of our engines, I screamed and screamed again, "Go back, Andy! Get out!"

Finally, with time running out, he realized that he could do nothing to help me. When I waved him away again, he hung his head and nodded, as though he was ashamed to leave—ashamed that sheer heart and courage hadn't been enough. Even then, Andy didn't turn his back on me. Instead, he crawled backward, through the fire again, never taking his eyes off me. On his face was a look of mute anguish.

When Andy reached the escape hatch again, he stood up. Slowly, as he'd so often done before in happier times together, he came to attention. Standing there in his flaming clothes, a grimly magnificent figure, he *saluted* me!

At the same time, just before he jumped, he said something. And though I couldn't hear, I knew it was "Good night, sir."

I turned, watched him fall away beneath the tail and saw his chute open. *So long, Irish. Good luck.*

Now I was alone. The Lanc was going down less steeply than before, but I knew it would hit the ground in a matter of seconds, with five tons of high explosives barely 50 feet from me. I curled up in the way prescribed for crash landings and waited for death.

Time froze. While I was struggling inside the turret and Andy was fighting to get me out alive, a minute or more had flashed by like a second. Now the last agonizing seconds were like eternity. Prayers and random thoughts raced through my mind. *Hail Mary, full of grace . . . God, I hope Andy got down okay . . . Pray for us sinners . . . "Brophy? Oh, he went for a Burton over Cambrai."*

Suddenly time caught up. Everything came at once—the ground's dark blur, the slam of a thousand sledgehammers, the screech of ripping metal. Just as the Lanc went bellying into a field, a thick tree slashed away its flaming port wing, spinning the plane violently to the left—its last dying lurch. *This is it.* But in that instant, at the last possible moment, the whiplash snapped my turret-prison open.

Without knowing it—for I'd blacked out—I was hurled through the air. When I came to a few seconds later, I heard two explosions. Only when I felt the solid, blessed earth tremble under me did I realize that the crash was over, and, somehow, I was alive.

Slowly, fearfully, I moved my arms and legs. Nothing hurt. Then I sat up. I wasn't even scratched! It was as if some gentle, unseen hand had swept me out of that hellish turret, now twisted and blazing a hundred feet away. Incredibly, and luckily for me, only two of the Lanc's 20 bombs had exploded.

But fear and horror had left their mark. For when I hauled off my helmet, most of my hair came with it.

After a night in hiding, I approached a farmer, who turned out to be a Resistance leader. With six other Allied airmen, I was passed through the French underground for 11 weeks, until British troops found us near Lens. All this time I kept seeking word of my crew-mates—especially Andy Mynarski.

When I got back to England, on September 13, I finally found out what had happened. Two of the crew had been taken prisoner; three others had got back via the underground. One of the latter was wireless operator Jim Kelly. After his parachute jump, Jim told me, a French farmer hid him in a barn. Soon another Frenchman arrived there. In halting English, he spoke of a parachutist who had landed alive, only to die of severe burns. Then he held out a flying helmet. Painted across the front was "Andy."

Almost numb with grief, I realized that Jim didn't know—no one else *could* know—why Andy died. I told the story to him, and later to air-force officials.

The RCAF document describing my escape as "miraculous" went on to say that Andy "must have been fully aware that in trying to free the rear gunner he was almost certain to lose his own life."

With that citation, Andrew Charles Mynarski was posthumously given the Victoria Cross, the British Commonwealth's highest award for valor. His portrait was hung in the National Gallery in Ottawa, and Winnipeg named a junior high school for this quiet young Canadian whose last act was a supreme triumph of the human spirit.

Only the second member of the RCAF to win the V.C., Andy was one of very few in history to get it on the uncorroborated testimony of a single witness. And I'll always believe that a divine providence intervened to save me because of what I had seen—so the world might know of a gallant man who laid down his life for a friend.

True friendship is a plant of slow growth,

and must undergo and withstand the

shocks of adversity before it is entitled to

the appellation.

GEORGE WASHINGTON

"OF TENDER HEART AND GENEROUS SPIRIT"

BY

DAVID REED

*E*very morning promptly at seven, the old man showed up at the eighteenth district police station on Chicago's Near North Side. He wore a cheap black hat pulled down to his eyes, a black raincoat shiny from wear, and a threadbare black suit. The soles of his boots were held on with rubber bands. Yet he was clean and always maintained a quiet dignity.

Taking a chair in the lobby, not far from the desk sergeant, the old man was surrounded by the continual uproar of citizens filing complaints, cops coming and going, and prisoners being brought in. He watched it all in silence, now and then nodding off. Then, at 11:00 A.M., he would leave without a word.

After six months, he had become a station fixture. "Just another bum," some cops said. But he never bothered anyone, so they left him alone.

Like everyone else, undercover cop Nick Kitowski assumed that the old man was a deaf mute. Then one November morning, Nick said hello to him. To the policeman's surprise, he responded with a friendly smile and a thumbs-up sign.

"Kinda chilly this morning," Nick said.

The old man leaned forward to hear better.

"See, he's hard of hearing, that's all," Nick told the others. Then he turned to the old man again. "What's your name?" Nick asked.

"George White." He said he lived on a Social Security pension and had a room in a nearby YMCA. He had just one shirt, which he washed in his room basin every evening and dried on the radiator. The old man came into the police station because he liked the excitement.

A bright, mustachioed, street-smart cop in his early thirties, Nick was used to thugs and bums of every description. He and his partner, Mitch Masalski, dressed in rough jackets, blue jeans and work boots. With guns tucked in their waistbands, they rode around in an unmarked car, ready to respond to any police emergency.

Some fellow cops called them Starsky and Hutch. Others who found Polish names difficult dubbed them the Ski Patrol. Nick would tell his wife and friends, "It's a thankless job. You don't experience bad things once. You experience them over and over again. It wears you down. You lose your faith in people."

Yet Nick found himself drawn to the old man. The next day he talked with him again. "How come you don't have a warm coat?" Nick asked.

The old man explained that two men had mugged him, taking his overcoat and the few coins in his pocket.

The Ski Patrol talked it over with other cops, and after collecting $75, they all bought George a new overcoat. "You look like a million dollars," Nick told him proudly.

But the next day the old man showed up without the coat. "I gave it to someone who needed it more than I do," he said sheepishly.

Following Nick's lead, more and more cops became friendly with the old man. A policewoman started calling him Grandpa and another one bought him warm gloves. Still others gave him food.

Once the old man told Nick and Mitch that he was seventy-nine years old. He said he came from Cleveland and that he had been a cross-country truck driver.

"If he wants to tell us more, he will," Nick said. But he never did.

Nick and Mitch began wondering where George went when he left the station each morning. So, being cops, they tailed him. The old man got on a bus and spent his afternoon riding from one end of the line to the other. Several times after that, as Nick and Mitch cruised the streets, they looked up at a passing bus and saw the old man in a window seat, lost in thought or nodding off on his endless journeys across the lonely city.

In December, Nick told the other cops he was planning to invite the old man to his home for Christmas dinner.

"Man, you've got to be out of your mind," one cop said. "He's a bum. He might have anything from beriberi to the plague."

"He's no bum—he's a gentleman," Nick said.

On Christmas Day, the Ski Patrol drove through the snowy streets of the city to pick up the old man at the YMCA. Nick's wife and two daughters made him feel like one of the family. They installed him in a comfortable chair, and the children brought him soft drinks. Everyone was won over by his shy smile.

When it came time to exchange gifts, Nick and Mitch gave the old man several gift-wrapped packages containing socks, toiletries, nuts and fruitcake. Nick asked the old man if he had any children. George didn't answer. Instead, he started crying.

That evening, Nick and Mitch drove the old man back to the YMCA. Along the way, he asked: "Are these presents really mine?"

"They sure are."

"Can I do anything I want with them?"

"No problem."

George put the gift wrapping back on the boxes and asked to be taken to the diner just around the corner from the police station. Nick and Mitch accompanied him inside. The old man handed his gifts to the owner, a man known as Billy the Greek.

"I want you to have these things," he said. "Merry Christmas."

"Gee, thanks," said Billy, taken aback.

George later explained that he seldom had enough money for a good meal and that, for the past year, Billy the Greek had been giving him breakfast—juice, eggs, bacon, toast and coffee—on the house. Billy would say only, "I like that old man."

When Nick and Mitch dropped the old man off at the YMCA, he shook their hands and said warmly, "I'll never, as long as I live, forget what you boys done for me this Christmas." Back in the car, Nick said, "George has really got class. I never met anyone like him before in my life."

Several months later, Nick came into the station late one morning and saw that George's chair was empty.

"Where's the old man?" he asked the desk sergeant.

"Don't know—he hasn't been in yet today."

When George failed to appear the next day as well, Nick and Mitch went to the YMCA. "He checked out and left no forwarding address," the manager said. "You know how it is with transients."

Eventually a street bum told Nick and Mitch that the old man had been taken to a hospital. They checked a dozen or so, but could find no trace of him.

Months went by, but neither Nick nor Mitch could forget the old man. As Christmas neared again, the Ski Patrol decided to retrace their steps. They went back to the YMCA and talked with a different manager. He knew nothing of George. As Nick and Mitch were turning to leave, a man who had overheard their conversation said, "Wait a minute. If you're talking about the guy with the black hat and black raincoat, you'll find him at the old people's home at Touhy and Western."

At the home, a nurse said the old man was in Columbus Hospital. "He's just had an operation on his stomach," the nurse explained. "It doesn't look so good for him."

Carrying presents of socks and candy, Nick arrived at the hospital on Christmas Eve. The old man had an oxygen mask on his face and tubes in his arm. His face lit up when he saw Nick. He smiled that shy, friendly smile of his and gave Nick the thumbs-up sign. Nick grabbed the old man's hand and shook it. "Merry Christmas, George," he said. "And God bless you."

Then the nurse swooshed him out of the room. "Please notify me if his condition changes," Nick said. He checked back by phone each day.

On New Year's Day, a nurse said, "I'm sorry, but Mr. White just passed away."

The old man would ordinarily have been buried as a pauper, with no mourners and no service. But when his hearse arrived at the cemetery, three men were waiting in the snow. Two wore rough street clothing and the third wore a clerical collar. Nick and Mitch had never asked the old man if he was a Catholic, but they thought it would be nice if a priest said prayers for him.

Father Jerry Scanlan of Saint Andrew's wondered what the old man had meant to police heavies like Nick and Mitch. "He reinforced my reason for becoming a policeman—to help people," Mitch said, hesitatingly. Nick added, "You really can't be certain about anything in this life. If I wind up sitting in a chair like George, maybe somebody will help me."

We secure our friends not by accepting favors but by doing them.

THUCYDIDES

One matter remained: the Ski Patrol wanted a proper tombstone. A monument company donated the stone, but the cemetery wanted $140 for a concrete footing. When Billy the Greek heard about it, he dipped into his cash register and proffered a handful of bills. Nick, Mitch and other cops came up with the rest.

Only Nick and Mitch ever visit the grave; only they know where it is. The tombstone has the old man's name and the date of his death; after these are the words: "Of tender heart and generous spirit."

ACKNOWLEDGMENTS

All the stories in *The Gift of Friendship* previously appeared in *Reader's Digest* magazine. We would like to thank the following contributors and publishers for permission to reprint material.

Ordeal on Killington Peak by Jon Vara. © 1992 by Jon Vara. Yankee (January '92).

Friends of the Road by Kim Shippey. © 1993 by Kim Shippey. The Christian Science Monitor (June 23, '93).

Neighbors by John Sherrill. Reprinted with permission from **Guideposts** magazine. Copyright © 1992 by Guideposts, Carmel, New York 10512.

A Dance I'll Never Forget by Hillary Hauser. © 1994 by Hillary Hauser. Santa Barbara News-Press (December 9, '95)

A Candle for Lori by Patricia Sherlock. © 1984 by Patricia Sherlock. Catholic Digest (October '84).

Send Someone a Smile by Ann Bateman. © 1982 by Ann Bateman. These Times (January '82).

I've Come to Clean Your Shoes by Madge Harrah. Reprinted with permission from **Guideposts** magazine. Copyright © 1981 by Guideposts, Carmel, New York 10512.

The Stranger Who Taught Magic by Arthur Gordon. © 1970 by Arthur Gordon.

A Kindness Returned by Virginia Hall Graves. Reprinted with permission from **Guideposts** magazine. Copyright © 1980 by Guideposts, Carmel, New York 10512.

Quotations

Roger Rosenblatt in Life (February 16, '98); *Pioneer Girls Leaders' Handbook; Merry Browne* in National Enquirer (December 6, '88); *Anais Nin* excerpt from THE DIARY OF ANAIS

Photo Credits

All photographs are from Photodisc unless otherwise credited below:

Carousel Research: Laurie Platt Winfrey, Van Bucher, Cristian Pena, Peter Tomlinson